Teaching and Preaching

High Holiday Bible Themes

Teaching and Preaching

A Resource Book

High Holiday Bible Themes

Volume I: Rosh Hashanah

Compiled by
Rabbi Sidney Greenberg

Hartmore House
New York & Bridgeport

The Editor wishes to express his gratitude to the following, whose copyrighted materials are included in this volume:

B'nai B'rith, for a passage from *May I Have a Word with You?* by Morris Adler; a passage from an article by Abraham J. Heschel published in the Spring-Summer 1971 issue of *Jewish Heritage*.

Ruth Brin, for "Abraham and Isaac" in *A Time to Search*.

Commentary, for a passage from "The Birthday of the World" by Ernst Simon, Copyright © 1955 by the American Jewish Committee.

Hartmore House, for passages from *Justice and Mercy* by Max Arzt; for passages from *The Fire Waits* by Michael I. Hecht; and for passages from *A Guide to Rosh Hashanah* by Louis Jacobs.

Houghton Mifflin Company, for a passage from *Last Things First* by Sydney J. Harris.

The Jewish Digest, for a passage from an article by Elie Wiesel, published in the September 1972 issue.

The Jewish Publication Society, for passages from *The Rosh Hashanah Anthology*, edited by Philip Goodman.

The Jewish Reconstructionist Foundation, for a passage from *The Meaning of God In Modern Jewish Religion* by Mordecai M. Kaplan.

Rabbi Herman Kieval, for passages from *The High Holy Days, Book I, Rosh Hashanah*, published by Burning Bush Press.

Rabbi Norman Lamm, for passages from *The Royal Reach*, published by Philip Feldheim, Inc.

Dr. Israel H. Levinthal, for a passage from *A New World Is Born*, published by Funk and Wagnalls.

Rabbi Joseph H. Lookstein, for passages from *Faith and Destiny of Man*, published by Bloch Publishing Company.

The Rabbinical Assembly, for a passage from Ernst Simon's article, "Torat Hayyim," published in the Spring 1958 issue of *Conservative Judaism*.

Random House, Inc., for a passage by Cecil Roth in *Great Ages and Ideas of the Jewish People*, edited by Leo W. Schwarz.

This volume, which brings together a variety of materials pertaining to the Torah and Haftarah readings of the High Holidays, is intended for use by rabbis and educators in planning sermons, "teaching commentaries," and discussions.

The *form* and *scope* of this book were suggested by Rabbi Jonathan D. Levine, who felt that the increased use of "teaching commentaries" at worship services (as well as the problems inherent in the use of entire sermons or discussion outlines prepared for other community settings) would make this new type of "working Resource Book" particularly useful at this time.

Rabbi Sidney Greenberg (whose earlier anthologies and homiletical books have become classics) was asked to undertake the editorship of the first volume in this "Teaching and Preaching" series. Since initial reactions to this manuscript for Rosh Hashanah have been most encouraging, Rabbi Greenberg has undertaken the editorship of a second volume for Yom Kippur which will be published next year.

Some of the material in this volume has been excerpted, digested, or adapted from previously published books and essays, while some of the material is new. But the *form* of the present volume is entirely new; we hope it will prove practical and helpful.

Generous margin space has been provided on each page—since this book is designed to be "worked on" rather than merely "looked at." By its nature, a volume of this kind cannot be all-inclusive. It can, however, provide a convenient source of useful material—to which additional items may be added over the years.

Reactions and suggestions to this book will be greatly appreciated and will be helpful in the compilation of subsequent volumes in this new series.

Erev Shavuot, 1973

DEDICATED WITH PRIDE AND GRATITUDE
TO THE
STATE OF ISRAEL
ON THE TWENTY-FIFTH ANNIVERSARY OF ITS INDEPENDENCE

CONTENTS

PROLOGUE

09/122

PROLOGUE:

Study of Torah as Worship

Seeds scattered but not tended often wither and produce no harvest. This might have been the fate of the practice of periodically reading and explaining scriptural selections at the informal worship periods during the Babylonian exile had it not been for the work of Ezra the Scribe. It was he who provided the powerful impetus that transformed the informal readings from the Torah into a central institution of Judaism.

Ezra was a Babylonian Jew who arrived in the Holy Land at the head of a second wave of emigrants. This took place in the year 458 B.C.E., seventy-five years after the first wave of emigrants in the days of King Cyrus. When Ezra arrived in Jerusalem he was shocked to find the Jewish community in a state of disintegration. The Bible tells us that he rent his garments, fasted, and prayed. Then he initiated a number of far-reaching reforms, the climax of which was launched at an assembly of the whole people to whom he read the Torah. This event is dramatically told in the Bible (Neh. 8:5-8):

> And Ezra opened the book in the sight of all the people . . . and when he opened it, all the people stood up. And Ezra blessed the Lord, the great God. And all the people answered, 'Amen, Amen' . . . And [Ezra and his associates] read in the book, in the Law of God, distinctly; and they gave the sense, and caused them to understand the reading.

The act of teaching the Torah to the whole people was a characteristic of Judaism from its very beginning. The Ten Commandments were given at Mount

5

Sinai to the whole assembly of Israel. In ancient times this was a revolutionary concept. In those days it was common practice for the priestly clans to be the custodians of the traditional knowledge and to keep this knowledge strictly to themselves. Judaism broke away from this practice and made the Torah available to all the people. To quote George Foot Moore, when Ezra introduced the public reading and teaching of the Torah as an element of worship, he introduced a process that

> has no parallel in the ancient Mediterranean world. The religion of the household in Egypt or Greece or Rome was a matter of domestic tradition, perpetuated by example rather than by instruction . . . ; the religion of the city or the state was a tradition of the priesthoods in whose charge the public cultus was . . . If the usage of the sanctuary was reduced to writing it was done privately or for the convenience of the priests themselves. The possession of a body of sacred Scriptures, including the principles of their religion as well as its ritual and the observances of the household and the individual, of itself put the Jews in a different case.*

The reading of the Torah in the synagogue service has developed a procedure which follows the precedent set by Ezra and his associates. To this day the scroll is unrolled and held up in the sight of the congregation, and the congregation rises as was done by the assemblage in Ezra's day: "And Ezra opened the book in the sight of all the people . . . and when he opened it, all the people stood up." As in the days of Ezra a benediction is recited before the reading: "And Ezra blessed the Lord, the great God. And all the people answered, 'Amen, Amen.' " The Torah is

*George Foot Moore, *Judaism in the First Centuries of the Christian Era* (Cambridge, Mass. 1927), 1:281.

read as it was read by Ezra and his associates—
"distinctly," in a distinctive traditional chant. The
"sense" used to be transmitted with the help of a
meturgeman, a translator, who stood near the reader
and translated each verse into the vernacular. The
teachers of the synagogue followed Ezra's example
and "caused [the people] to understand" the Torah
through explanations and homilies.

Ezar not only set the pattern for reading the Torah
at public services on Sabbaths and festivals, but he
also brought the Torah to the people at other
convenient occasions. He introduced the custom of
reading the Torah on Mondays and Thursdays, when
the farmers used to come to town to sell their
produce and to purchase their household goods.*
Mondays and Thursdays are no longer market days,
but the custom instituted by Ezra has persisted to
this day: The Torah is still read regularly at Monday
and Thursday morning services.

—Abraham E. Millgram

*Soferim 10:1.

ON THE TORAH READINGS FOR
THE HIGH HOLY DAYS

Rosh Hashanah and Yom Kippur differ from the other festivals of the Jewish calendar in many ways. A basic difference is that—unlike Pesah, Shavuot, Sukkot, Purim and Hanukkah—they have *no connection with Jewish history!*

1. There is nothing wrong with this, of course. Indeed, we have cause to rejoice because Rosh Hashanah and Yom Kippur are truly *universal in their religious appeal.* These days of Judgment and Remembrance, Repentance, and Atonement speak to the human, as well as to the Jewish, situation. Nevertheless, our ancestors in Eretz Yisrael and Babylonia, almost 2,000 years ago, were not entirely happy that these Days of Penitence had no direct association with the specific historical experience of the Jewish people. So they tried to remedy the situation. How did they go about this?

2. In the case of Rosh Hashanah, the Sages actually *changed the original Torah readings!* As we know from the Mishnah (Megillah 3:5*), the portion originally read was the section from the classic list of the festivals in Leviticus 23 that deals with the first day of the seventh month. These few verses (23-25) are purely ritualistic in content. But by the time of the Talmud, this practice had been changed and new Torah passages substituted (see Megillah 31a).

---

*Tosefta Megillah 3:6, ed. Lieberman, p. 354 records a divergence of practice: some read Gen. 21:1-34, others read Lev. 23. But Gen. 22, as a reading for Rosh Hashanah, is not found in Tannaitic sources.

3. The new readings are chapters 21 and 22 of Genesis, which we still read on the two days of Rosh Hashanah respectively. These passages constitute a narrative describing key events in the life of the patriarch Abraham and thus represent the observance of Rosh Hashanah.* Since Rosh Hashanah is called the Day of Remembrance, *Yom Ha-Zikkaron*, the first day's reading begins with the words "Now God *remembered* Sarah," to give her a son in her old age. The entire passage closes with the spiritual climax of Abraham's career, the drama of the Binding of Isaac.

Why was Rosh Hashanah associated historically by later Jewish tradition with the career of Abraham? There is much speculation over this question, but the reason would seem to be the obvious one: because *Abraham is the founding father of the Jewish people and God's Covenant was made with him.*

1. The opening chapters of the Bible may be described as God's search for a righteous man, and His repeated disappointment: in Adam and his progeny, in Noah and his descendants. But the Creator offered mankind another chance to succeed.

2. This time, however, God placed His trust, not in any one individual, but in a family that was to grow into a great and consecrated nation. Yet every family starts with one man and that man was Abraham our Father.

—Herman Kieval

*CF. Leon J. Liebreich: "Aspects of the New Year Liturgy", in *HUCA*, vol. XXXIV, 1963, pp. 137, 147.

FIRST DAY OF ROSH HASHANAH

GOD, THE TRUSTEE

The Bible teaches that "The Lord took note of Sarah as He had promised, and the Lord did for Sarah as He had spoken" (Genesis 21:1). The Midrash quotes Rabbi Adda as saying that God is a trustee, Who returns whatever is deposited with Him. Because Sarah accumulated a store of good deeds, the Lord returned these to her in the form of a reward.

Whatever we get is paid for either in advance or afterward. Usually the good things in life are paid for in advance, while the bad things are paid for afterward. Love is paid for in advance by sacrifice and service. Lust is paid for afterward by remorse and regret. Peace is paid for in advance by mutual trust. War is paid for afterward by lifeless cities and broken bodies. That which is deposited is eventually returned for good or for evil.

Many years ago a wealthy family in England took the children for a holiday into the country. Their host, a gardener, turned over his estate for the week-end to the visitors. When the children went swimming in the pool, one of the boys fell in and began to drown. The other boys screamed for help, and the son of the gardener jumped into the pool and rescued the helpless one. Later, the grateful parents asked the gardener what they could do for the youthful hero. The gardener said that his son wanted to go to college some day. "He wants to be a doctor," said the gardener. The visitors shook hands on that. "We'll be glad to pay his way through," they said.

When Winston Churchill was stricken with pneumonia after the Teheran Conference, the King of England instructed the best doctor to be found to save the Prime Minister. That doctor turned out to be Alexander Fleming, the developer of penicilin. Later Churchill said, "Rarely has one man owed his life twice to the same rescuer." It was Sir Alexander who saved Churchill in that pool!

—*Saul Teplitz*　　13

GOD REMEMBERS: *cf. Genesis 21:1*

The prelude to the *Zikhronot* asserts that there appears before God "the record of every man's deeds, his works and his ways, his thoughts and his schemes, his plans, and the motives of his acts." It further afffirms, "Happy is the man who forgets Thee not and the son of man who finds strength in Thee." This unquestioning faith enabled the Jew to face the future with courage, in the most trying circumstances. His endurance and strength were derived from the belief that God "surveys and sees all that happens to the end of all generations." Rather than presume to sit in judgment over God's government of the world, he chose to subject his own life to God's scrutiny. To know that God did not abdicate His rule once He created the world, nor that God abandoned man to blind fate and random chance, was to him sufficient reason so to live as to merit God's merciful "remembrance." The faith expressed in the prelude to the *Zikhronot* can be for us, as well, a faith for confident and courageous living. Our inability to plot the curve of retribution and reward in the unfolding of history should not dampen our belief in God's providence. Regardless of the individual's personal fortunes, God's "remembrance" of our deeds of virtue and valor redeems our life from meaninglessness by validating our struggles for the enthronement of the moral law in the life of all men.

The last of the *Zikhronot* verses, "I will for their sakes remember the covenant of their ancestors, whom I brought forth out of the land of Egypt in the sight of the nations, that I might be their God: I am the Lord" (Lev. 26:45), is integrated into the blessing of this section. Envisioning Israel's future redemption, the *Zikhronot* section reaches a climactic conclusion as it refers to the *Akedah*, the prototype and the symbol of merit and moral example accumulated for the Jew by the martyred heroes of the past.

—Max Arzt

Torah Reading:
First Day of
Rosh Hashanah

For the Jew, memory is known by another name. That name is tradition.

For many, memory is a flashback from the past; to us it is a hand-down from the past for the endless future of our people. Others merely recall; we receive.

"Remember the Sabbath day to keep it holy." This is a command to remember. But is it only that? Of course, the Sabbath is a lovely, a romantic, even a dramatic memory—a clean tablecloth, candles, traditional dishes, perhaps even a family melody. Let no one minimize that. At best, however, this is merely a Sabbath—Jewish style. But the Sabbath, in addition to being remembered, must be observed. It is a day of rest, a day of holiness, a day in the course of which man transforms himself from mere creature to human being and from human being to Jew. Our sages would have us believe that when, at Sinai, God commanded, "Remember the Sabbath day to keep it holy," those who were there simultaneously heard a voice, which said, "Observe the Sabbath and sanctify it . . . "* Remember and Observe! Memory became tradition.

"Remember the day that you left Egypt." Again we are bidden to remember. This time we are asked to recall bondage, suffering, indignity and a host of other misfortunes that are the portion of a slave people. But here, too, that isn't all. The memory of Egypt imposes a commitment to freedom, a concern for the downtrodden, an interest in the enslaved, an eagerness to "proclaim liberty throughout the land and to all the inhabitants thereof." Here we have memory at work. When that happens, memory becomes tradition.

When children in Tennessee have to be led to school under guard of bayonets, the heart of a Jew is stirred. When the temple of education, the most precious sanctuary of democracy, is defiled by

*R.H. 27a.

segregation and polluted by discrimination, then the Jew, whether Northerner or Southerner, ought not to rest without exerting every effort to cleanse and to purify the minds and the hearts of his fellow Americans. To recall Egypt, that is memory. To abolish all the Egypts, now and forever, that is the command of tradition.

"Remember the day when you stood before your God at Sinai." What a magnificent drama took place there. There was thunder and lightning and all the sound effects known and not yet known to modern impresarios. A people stood in awe, shook and shuddered before a spectacle of Revelation never previously performed, never to be repeated. But what took place at Sinai was more than a memory to be deposited in the mental archives of a people. There was an exclamation, "We shall do and we shall listen." By that act of commitment the memory became a tradition, binding upon the Jew to all eternity.

> *"Hail, Memory, hail! in thy exhaustless mine*
> *From age to age unnumber'd treasures shine!*
> *Thought and her shadowy brood thy call obey,*
> *And Place and Time are subjects to thy sway."**

This is a poet's insight into memory. This, indeed, is memory transmuted from vision to action, from hindsight to foresight, from dream to reality.

O for the art of memory! Almighty God, on this Day of Remembrance, among all the other blessings, grant us this one—never to forget to remember.

—*Joseph H. Lookstein*

*Rovers: *Pleasures of Memory.*

16

The Torah reading for Rosh Hashanah begins with the birth of one little boy. The name of the boy is Isaac. He was extremely important to the development of Judaism. God had promised Abraham that He would make his name great and that he would be the father of a mighty multitude, as numerous as the sands of the sea and the stars of heaven. His descendants would be enlisted in Divine service, teaching men to believe in the One God, the God of justice and mercy and truth.

But this entire promise hinged upon one little boy; for without that child to carry the message and the commitment there would be no future. One little boy was the key to tomorrow and to all the centuries between Abraham and ourselves.

Significantly, the Haftarah for this morning deals also with the birth of one little boy. The name of the boy was Samuel who was to leave an enormous imprint upon Jewish thought and life through the two books of our Bible which bear his name and reflect the passion of the first of the great prophets after Moses.

Isn't it strange, when we stop to think of it, that both the Torah reading and the Haftarah should focus so sharply upon the single individual precisely on Rosh Hashanah where our concern seems to be with the whole world? *"Hayom Harat Olam*—on this day the world came into being." Our scope on this day is as wide as the whole universe.

"And therefore, O Lord our God, let Your awe be manifest in all Your works and a reverence for You fill *all* that You have created so that *all* Your creatures may know You and *all* mankind bow down to acknowledge You."

17

On Rosh Hashanah the canvas is the entire world and the subject is all mankind and yet the Torah reading and the Haftarah reading each talk about one little boy.

There is enormous wisdom compressed into this preoccupation of Rosh Hashanah with the solitary individual. For our purposes I would like to call attention to *three* specific implications which have direct and immediate relevance to us in our time.

In the first place, it drives home to us the fundamental Jewish teaching that every human being is unique.

There is a second vital lesson in Rosh Hashanah's preoccupation with the lone human being. It underscores not only the uniqueness of each person but also the sanctity of each person. Every human being is a whole world in himself.

By focusing upon the single individual, Rosh Hashanah reminds us also of our power. You and I have extraordinary capacities and all kinds of latent force. We each have the power to transform our lives. We can each make a decisive difference in the world.

—Sidney Greenberg

LAUGHTER SILENCED TO WONDER

The name *Isaac* is connected in this and in other Biblical passages with the Hebrew root *tzahak* meaning 'to laugh.' In the context this has the connotation of 'mocking laughter.' To their contemporaries, even to themselves, there was something absurd about the birth of a child to Abraham and Sarah, this man and woman of advanced years. Jewish teachers have read into the account an anticipation of the fate of Isaac's descendants, the people of Israel. The very birth of this people was a miracle, who but a Moses, under divine aid, could have succeeded in welding a rabble of slaves into a great nation? In subsequent Jewish history it seemed on more than one occasion that the Jews were doomed to extinction. The mocking laughter which attended the birth of Isaac re-echoed at the destruction of the first and second Temples, at the expulsion from Spain, and, in our own day, in Nazi-dominated Europe. But always the laughter was silenced to wonder as bruised Israel survived to rebuild its life in new surroundings.

—Louis Jacobs

METZACHEK

"Cast out this bondswoman and her son; for the son of this bondswoman shall not be heir with my son, even with Isaac."

This is one of the most perplexing stories in the whole Bible. Mother Sarah, according to our teaching, was the personification of human goodness and kindliness. How could she be guilty of such inconsiderateness, of such apparent cruelty? What was Ishmael's crime that she should call for such punishment? *Metzachek*, that is all that the Bible tells us. Evidently, there is something deeper in the meaning of that word than the ordinary English translation would lead us to believe. Surely, Mother Sarah would not stand aghast simply at the sight of the two boys *playing* with each other and laughing in their enjoyment.

You may recall that her son's name Isaac was derived from the word *Tzachok*, meaning "laughter" —*Yitzchak*, literally, "He will laugh," "He will find joy." It is strange, but this word, too—*Metzachek* —comes from the same root *Tzachok*, "to laugh." *Yitzchak* and *Metzachek*—there seems to be a conflict between these two words, both derived from the same source! There is evidently a clash between the laughter of Isaac and the laughter of Ishmael, between the joys derived by the one and the joys derived by the other. When Sarah's son was named *Yitzchak*, it was the vision and the hope of his parents that he would laugh and find joy in the ideals of the godly life that he would inherit from his parents. "He will laugh" the laughter of joy in carrying high the banner of the new faith proclaimed by 'Abraham. Of Ishmael, too, the Bible says that *Metzachek*—"he laughed." But his laughter comes from an altogether different cause; he derives his joy from something that strikes horror in sensitive souls.

The sages in the Midrash understood this story in all its significance. "What is the real meaning of the word *Metzachek*, as here used?" they ask. And three Rabbis offer their answers, each giving Biblical citations as proof of the correctness of his definition. Rabbi Ishmael said: *En Ha-lashon Hazeh Shel Tzachok, Elo Avoda Zara*, "This word really means idolatry. Mother Sarah saw him setting up strange altars and finding hilarious joy and laughter as he offered sacrifices to idols." R. Eliezer said: "This word as here used means *Shefikhat Damim*, murder!" The watchful mother would observe this lad hiding behind trees, and finding sport in aiming his bow and arrow at innocent passers-by. What laughter would come to him if his aim proved good, and he beheld the blood of his human target! And R. Akiba said: "This word as used in our text means *Gilui Arayot, the revealing of his naked immoralities.*" He would daringly capture young girls, rape them, and laugh at the helplessness and misery of his victims!

Now, we begin to understand the fright of Mother Sarah as she noted that Ishmael was endeavoring to teach this laughter to her son Isaac. We can see why this kindly soul should make so grave a demand, and have the courage to insist: Drive him away, cast him out, for he shall not be heir with my son, with Isaac! There can be no sharing of fate between the two—between the laughter of an Ishmael and the laughter of an Isaac!

—Israel H. Levinthal

TO REMAIN HUMAN
IN FACE OF INHUMANITY

A young soldier had accepted to go on a suicide mission across the Suez Canal. Every night the operation was postponed for technical reasons, until it was cancelled altogether. Only then did the kibbutz-born, kibbutz-educated soldier—named Isaac —realize what it meant to be a survivor; he felt like the first Isaac must have felt after the Test. And he began to study all the material relevant to the Akeda—following in this respect, too, the son of Abraham. Doesn't the Midrash teach us that after leaving Mount Moriah, Isaac—the first holocaust survivor in Jewish history—went into retreat to study Torah?

Let us talk about Isaac. Let us repeat his tale, which is our tale. For his experience is ours and so is his anguish and perhaps his triumph as well.

The meaning of the name Isaac, in Hebrew —Yitzchak—is: he who will laugh. Strange: for the most tragic figure in Jewish history, to have been given such a bizarre name! The man who saw his father almost turn murderer, the man who saw God almost become victim of his own cruelty—and he will "laugh?" Laugh at whom? And why? What was there—what is there—to laugh about?

Yet the name Isaac is related to the future, hence the dominant role laughter has played in our history, a history in which past and future are interchangeable. More than 3,000 years separate the Isaac on Moriah from the Isaac waiting at Suez, yet they are both our contemporaries. We think we're inventing new tales? It is always the same old one told and retold over and over again—so why shouldn't it be cause for laughter? Normally, logically, Isaac and his descendants should have, at one point or another, put an end to their tale so burdened with agony—why didn't they?

Following the destruction of the second Temple, the Jewish people had two options before them, and both have been recorded. The first: to go under. *Nitrabu haprushim be-Yisrael*: more and more men, drained by mourning, decided never to marry, as though to tell God: if that's the way you want it, if you prefer a world without Jews or else with Jews closed to joy, so be it! They were determined not to bring any more children into such a world. But the people overruled them, by deciding on the second option: to go on and build upon the ruins, and the greater the ruins, the more beautiful the House. And out of the Temple, in flames, came a tale of hope, the most magnificent tale of all, a work of art: the Talmud.

Where did Rabbi Yohanan ben Zakkai find the courage to begin a new era in history? Where did the Rabbis find the strength to believe that the Talmud would survive, that there would be Jews to teach it and Jews to study it, or even that there would be Jews left at all? Rejected by God, humiliated by men, the Jewish people had every reason in the world to despair, to accept defeat and give up new dreams. Was that a time for erecting new structures and proclaiming the Law?

I submit, the Talmud was conceived and written as an act of defiance. As though the Sages wished to tell God then and there: You want us to concede? To give in? We refuse! You want us to exit from history, you even want us not to record it. We refuse! Even if it be Thy will that we do not continue, we shall not abide by it! We shall believe in Israel—in spite of you!

Their stance did but confirm the ancient message of Judaism, namely: while man cannot begin—only God can do that!—it is given to man not to accept an imposed end. To begin is not in the realm of man's possibilities; only to begin again, over and over again—and therein lies his strength.

And his pride, too.

The same element of defiance, as a motivating force for national survival, is to be found throughout subsequent centuries; it dominates our entire body of martyrology.

For many reasons, both personal and professional. I delve into the sources in order to study my predecessors' techniques. So anxious am I to learn how they dealt with suffering, that I try to read every volume published on the subject. And sometimes I am seized with a mad desire to laugh and cry in bewilderment! Disregard the names of places, or people, specific dates, the story is always the same. And you begin to consider which is more baffling: the obstinacy of the executioner in wanting to destroy Jewish life, or the stubborness of the Jew in wanting to survive.

You read books from the medieval period such as *Shevet Yehudah* or *Emek Habacha*: tales of tears and whales of tales. You read of entire communities wiped out by invaders' crusaders, avenging armies. Centers of learning, great and small, obliterated overnight. Another enemy come and gone, another Jewish community apparently dead, and yet, 24 hours later, the community comes back to life. We know from the same sources that hardly had the enemy left, when out of the ashes emerged men and women, promptly engaging in Halahic or ritual discussions as to what should be rebuilt first — the cemetery or the synagogue?

You read these stories, and sooner or later you cannot but wonder: why did so many victims of so many tragedies go on proclaiming their faith? Why didn't they quit? Why didn't they choose to end their suffering and the suffering of their children by converting — assimilating — dissolving into society? They could have. Certainly as individuals. But they didn't. Why?

A story is narrated in *Shevet Yehudah* about Jews who fled their village, their country. They boarded a ship which eventually they had to abandon. They landed on a desert. Hunger, thirst, disease befell

24

them; many died. Among them was a pious man whose wife had died of hunger. He continued his march, hoping to reach a Jewish settlement. His two children were too weak, so he carried them. They, too, died and he went on carrying them. When he finally realized that he was the last survivor, the pain was so sharp he fainted. When he came to, he looked around first, and then he looked up to the sky and addressed God: Master of the Universe, I know what you want; you want me to stop believing in you — but you won't succeed, you hear me, you won't succeed!

This tale — of extraordinary beauty and power — makes its nameless hero our contemporary. His words could have been uttered by any one of the survivors when speaking to God of His creation. During and after the Holocaust, it was impossible for any Jew not to choose defiance as a means of transcending despair.

What happened some 25 years ago, cannot and will not — and perhaps should not — be recorded. For what happened goes beyond words, beyond imagination. To make words of it would be blasphemous. Rabbi Mendel of Kotzk said: Truth can sometimes be communicated by words though there is a level of Truth so deep it can be conveyed only by silence. And then, lastly, there is somewhere in a man a Truth so profound and so disturbing, it cannot be transmitted at all. The Holocaust must then be placed in this last category.

I don't want, I never did want, to sadden you with tales of the Holocaust. To the contrary: I had hoped when writing, not novels but pages of testimony, that I would succeed somehow in provoking laughter not tears. When asked what kind of a museum he would erect in Auschwitz if it were up to him, German novelist Guenther Grass answered: a circus! He, too, wants to make people laugh because of Auschwitz. Only his concept of laughter is not mine; his is the

25

clown's laughter; mine is the madman's. The madman is always present in my tales; he laughs and laughs, yet he cannot make others laugh with him, like him. He is my model. He and not those who cry and lament. I don't believe in madness. I believe in joy, in ecstasy, especially when they are beyond our reach. This may sound sacrilegious to you: one can, one must speak—even of the Holocaust—with joy, with ecstasy, with laughter.

Those of you who want to understand, have understood by now: I am not speaking of the past but of the present. In other words, I am asking you now, what are you doing with our past?

I remember: April 1945. Buchenwald. Liberated at last. Twenty thousand inmates on one side, the entire world on the other. When the first American jeeps appeared at the gates, there were no outbursts of joy; the inmates did not have the strength to rejoice. They looked and looked at their liberators; they looked but they could not see; their eyes still held the image of the 60,000 prisoners taken away the preceding week. Then, something happened: a few Russian POW's grabbed some jeeps and machine-guns and raced to Weimar, the neighboring town and opened fire at will. That was their first gesture as free men. They needed vengeance before they needed food.

And what did the Jewish inmates do to prove they were free? Believe it or not; they held services. To give thanks to God? No, to defy him! To tell him: listen, as mere mortals, as members of the human society, we know we should seize weapons and use them in every place and in every way and never stop—because it is our right. But we are Jews and as such we renounce that right; we choose—yes, choose—to remain human. And generous.

Is there no message in this tale? Is this not the message of Jewish tradition? To remain human even in the face of inhumanity?

—Elie Wiesel

WHERE HE IS

There is a significant *Midrashic* comment on the verse: "God heard the voice of the lad where he is." The *Midrash* imagines the angels protesting: "How can Ishmael be spared in that his descendants will torment Israel?" God replies: "At this moment he is worthy to be saved"; God hears the voice of the lad *where he is*. Man is a creature of moods and cannot live ever on the heights. The firm resolves he makes on *Rosh Ha-Shanah* may weaken when the days of self-examination are gone. But at least, the Rabbis might have said, let man's purpose be strong on these days that God might hear his voice *where he is*.

—Louis Jacobs

HAGAR

Lone in the wilderness, her child and she,
   Sits the dark beauty, and her fierce-eyed boy.
A heavy burden and no winsome toy
To such as she, a hanging babe must be.
A slave without a master-wild, nor free,
With anger in her heart! and in her face
Shame for foul wrong and undeserved disgrace,
Poor Hagar mourns her lost virginity!
Poor woman fear not—God is everywhere;
The silent tears, thy thirsty infant's moan,
Are known to Him whose never-absent care
Still wakes to make all hearts and souls his own;
He sends an angel from beneath his throne
To cheer the outcast in the desert bare.

—Hartley Coleridge,
"Hagar"

27

JEWS

How came they here? What burst of Christian hate,
  What persecution merciless and blind,
Drove over the sea—that desert desolate—
  These Ishmaels and Hagars of mankind?

> *—Henry W. Longfellow,*
> "The Jewish Cemetery at Newport"

"And she went and sat down . . . a good way off, as it were a *bowshot*."

"And he became an *archer*."

The metaphor of a bowshot in the mind of the parent is illustrated of her universe of discourse. Her vision was about a "bow shot", and so later the Bible is able to record of Ishmael that he became an archer.

Question. What life styles do we show to our children by our vision, by our behavior and even by our speech?

> *—Chaim Pearl*

NO CRY UNANSWERED

No appeal to God, no cry of distress, goes unanswered. "God hears a cry of sorrow even when it is unuttered," said Rabbi Mendel. Commenting on the verse "And God heard the voice of the lad," he explained it in this way: "Nothing in the preceding verses indicates that Ishmael cried out. No, it was a soundless cry, but God heard it."

> *—Sidney Greenberg*

28

And God opened her eyes and she saw a well of water; and she went and filled the bottle with water, and gave the lad drink."

Let us note carefully what the Torah tells us about Hagar's deliverance. God did not create a well in answer to her desperate prayers. The well had been there all along. Her source of salvation and survival was close at hand. What God did for Hagar was to open her eyes so that she saw the well, the obvious she had overlooked.

How I wish that God would do for us what He did for Hagar—simply open our eyes to the unnumbered glories that surround us, the extravagant beauty that enfolds us, the manifold blessings which sustain us. If only we could see the obvious, what an effective antidote that would be to our gnawing discontent, our insatiable ambitions, our quiet desperation, our restless nights, our parched days. God has placed us in a Garden of Eden and instead of feeding upon its varied delights, we are forever drawn to the apple He placed off limits. So preoccupied are we with what we lack that we are unmindful of what we possess. A well-known English author and critic reminded us of this when he wrote: "I am not surprised at what men suffer but I am surprised at what men miss."

The newspapers recently carried a touching story of a mother who was taking her little son to Salt Lake City on a melancholy mission. The boy had lost the sight of one eye several years previous and in the intervening years, medical men had tried valiantly to save his remaining eye. Now they had come to the reluctant conclusion that the eye could not be saved. Before the darkness set in, his mother wanted the boy to have a fond lingering look at the majestic mountains of Utah so that he could take that splendid image with him into the sightless future. Can we read such a story without becoming acutely aware of the myriad marvels which constantly beckon to us and which we persistently overlook precisely because they are so many and so obvious?

—Sidney Greenberg

TAKE THE TIME TO SEE FOR REAL

STARBUCK, the dreamer of dreams that almost never come true, complains to Lizzie about a world in which reality falls far short of a man's vision.

STARBUCK: . . . Nothing's as pretty in your hands as it was in your head. There ain't no world near as good as the world I got up here (angrily tapping his forehead). Why?

LIZZIE: I don't know. Maybe it's because you don't take time to see it. Always on the go—here, there, nowhere. Running away . . . keeping your own company. Maybe if you'd keep company with the *world* . . .

STARBUCK: (*doubtfully*) I'd learn to love it?

LIZZIE: You might—if you saw it *real*. Some nights I'm in the kitchen washing the dishes. And Pop's playing poker with the boys. Well, I'll watch him real close. And at first I'll just see an ordinary middle-aged man—not very interesting to look at. And then, minute by minute, I'll see little things I never saw in him before. Good things and bad things—queer little habits I never noticed he had—and ways of talking I never paid any mind to. And suddenly I know who he is—and I love him so much I could cry! And I want to thank God I took the time to see him real.

—N. Richard Nash,
in "The Rainmaker"

GOD OPENED HER EYES AND SHE SAW

The literary critic and writer, Edmund Wilson, was in Israel and in Jordan after the six-day war. In an article in The New Yorker soon after the war, he described his impressions of both the old and the new sections of Jerusalem. "The ancient monuments themselves," he wrote, "with the exception of the Mosque of Omar, are not of remarkable beauty. The Wailing Wall, so important to the Jews, is not in itself impressive."

I am not at all surprised at the slight impression which this sacred monument of stone made upon him. A non-Jew, gazing at this Wall, sees nothing but massive blocks of stone—one upon the other,— without decoration or particular artistic beauty. But, a Jew, looking at this wall, sees more than the actual bare stones. He sees 3000 years of history; he sees the glory of the magnificent Temple built by Solomon; he sees the destruction of that Temple by the Babylonians; he sees the second Temple rebuilt by the Judean returnees of the captivity, and he sees its destruction by the Romans. He sees the one desolate, remaining wall of that ancient glory, before which for 1900 years, he poured out his heart in tearful prayer for the return of his people to that Golden City of his hope—Jerusalem—of which that bare wall was its inspiring symbol.

From the point of view of sheer architecture certainly the Mosque of Omar, still resplendent in all its original beauty, is far more impressive. A non-Jew contrasting the bare wall of massive stones with this Moslem structure, would of course see more splendor in the latter. He cannot see the Wall with the same eyes with which a Jew beholds it. No wonder that even the religiously non-observant Jew, when approaching this Wall, would embrace it with his arms and kiss it with his lips, because he saw much more in it than the non-Jew. He saw in this Wall thousands of years of his people's history; he heard from that Wall the voices of his prophets, psalmists and sages; above all, he heard as he looked at these stones, the wails and cries of a tortured people throughout the centuries, who, nevertheless, never gave up the hope to see it again.

Professor Abraham J. Heschel, the modern prophetic voice of our people, put it beautifully in his article on "An Echo of Eternity," which appeared in a recent issue of the Hadassah magazine: "The Wall. The old mother crying for all of us. Stubborn, loving, waiting for redemption. . . . All of our history is waiting here.

"The Wall. No comeliness to be acclaimed, no beauty to be relished. But a heart and an ear, its very being is compassion. What is the Wall? The unceasing marvel. Expectation."

No non-Jew, not even a great literary figure like Edmund Wilson, can see in these stones what the Jew sees in them, nor is he able to hear from these stones the messages of comfort and hope which reach the ear of the Jew standing before it.

And this is true also of Jerusalem,—especially the old Jerusalem which has now returned to the Jew. The nations of the world cannot understand this mystic bond which ties the Jew to that holy city. It is something more than just the capital of his ancient homeland. It is something more than Paris is to the Frenchman, or London to the Englishman, or Washington to the American.

It is the city from which the voice of the Prophets were heard; the city that gave the world the vision of universal peace and human brotherhood. It is the city which the Jew, in all his travail, never forgot, and to which he gave his constant pledge: "If I forget thee,

33

O Jerusalem, let my right hand forget its cunning." It is the city towards which he turned whenever he prayed.

Again, to quote the words of Professor Heschel: "For so many ages, we have been love-sick. 'My beloved is mine, and I am his,' Jerusalem whispered. We waited unbearably long, frustration and derision. In our own days, the miracle occurred. Jerusalem has proclaimed loudly: 'My beloved is mine, and I am his!' "

—Israel H. Levinthal

Samuel Jonson once remarked that "the two most engaging powers of an author are to make new things familiar and familiar things new." His statement points up the two varying (though complementary) functions of science and religion. The first seeks to confer the assurance and satisfaction that knowledge of the world about us yields. We are uneasy in the presence of the strange and the unpredictable. They spell mystery and to some degree danger. The unknown intrigues our curiosity and inspires restlessness within us.

One of the finest attributes of the human mind is its insatiable hunger to know and understand the world. Our feeling of at-homeness in the physical universe grows with our increasing grasp of the forces and laws that operate within it. Thus science brings the hitherto uncomprehended into the ken of our knowledge. It makes the world a "familiar" place, and thus enables us to live in greater peace and security within it.

Religion's task is the converse. It aims to have us live with an unfailing sense of wonderment and excitement. Every sight which our eyes behold, every breath we draw, and every encounter we experience are charged with mystery and depth. The laws that operate in the universe—are they not marvels of infinite wonder? The sun rising every morning is a tribute to an order beyond the ability of the human mind fully to fathom. The stars in their courses sing hymns of praise to the Cosmic Poet in whose mind they first arose as thoughts, even as "the heavens declare the glory of God and the firmament shows His handiwork."

Our growing knowledge should augment our awareness of the wonders about us. The man of faith seeing the hand of God in all that transpires is constantly agitated by the unending procession of divine manifestations everywhere he turns. The mind within us that thinks, the heart that feels—are they less wondrous than the mountains on earth or the constellations in heaven? There is a universe of wonder within us. The passing days and moving years are themselves enchanting fragments of an eternity beyond human reckoning.

Nothing is commonplace in a world over which the spirit of God hovers. A universe which renews itself daily has no room in it for the dull and commonplace. The Psalmist prays, "Open Thou mine eyes that I may behold wondrous things. . . ." Only he whose eyes are closed and whose heart has hardened will fail to recognize that he is participant in and spectator of a cavalcade of daily wonders. For in the world of faith everything is new and wonders never cease.

—Morris Adler

ONLY HE WHO SEES . . .

The greatest thing a human soul ever does in this world is to see something. Hundreds of people can talk to one who can think, but thousands can think for one who can see. To see clearly is poetry, prophecy, and religion all in one.

—John Ruskin

Earth's crammed with heaven,
And every common bush afire with God;
But only he who sees, takes off his shoes,
The rest sit round it and pluck blackberries.

—Elizabeth Barrett Browning

It is more difficult to teach the ignorant to think than it is to teach an intelligent blind man to see the grandeur of Niagara. I have walked with people whose eyes are full of light, but who see nothing in woods, sea, or sky, nothing in the city street, nothing in books. What a witless masquerade is this seeing:

It were better far to sail forever
In the night of blindness
With sense and feeling and mind
Than to be thus content with the mere act of
seeing.

They have the sunset, the morning skies, the purple of distant hills, yet *their souls voyage through this enchanted world with nothing but a barren stare.*

—Helen Keller

37

AS YOU REMEMBERED SARAH

Genesis 21:12

"The Lord remembered Sarah as He had promised;
The Lord did for Sarah as He had spoken:

"Sarah conceived and bore Abraham a son
In his old age."

And then nothing was simple anymore.
It was easier to become a mother
Than to be one.

It was easier to hope for the impossible
Than to accept the challenge
Of her dream fulfilled.

Her son grew,
Bringing more dreams,
More desires,
More pain.

"Thank You, God, for my son.
Now may I live to wean him . . .
Thank You, God, for letting me wean him.
Now help me raise him to be loyal . . .
Thank You, God, for all that is good in my son.
Now help me find him a wife . . . "

God, remember us
As You remembered Sarah,
Replacing old desires
With new hopes.

Today we pray for life.
Today we ask for health and prosperity.
Give us these things.
But do not give us quiet hearts.

For quiet begins in the grave,
The end of pain
And the end of hope.

*Torah Reading:
First Day of
Rosh Hashanah*

Keep our dreaming unfulfilled.
Give us ever-new hopes
And the strength for ever-new worries.

Remember us
As You remembered Sarah.

Give us life
And life's new problems.

—Michael Hecht

39

FROM GREY TO GOLD

cf. Genesis 21:9

The peanut is one of the humble products in the granary of nature. But in the hands of a scientist such as George Washington Carver, it was revealed to be infinitely rich in all kinds of possibilities. From peanuts he made a dozen beverages, mixed pickles, instant and dry coffee, tan remover, wood filler, paper, ink, shaving cream, linoleum, and synthetic rubber. Things are not always what they seem at first. By exploring beneath the surface we often discover that what we judged of little worth really contains hidden treasures waiting to be claimed by man.

We have often dismissed life as valueless because we did not probe it deeply enough. In our friends, in our children, in ourselves, lie dormant all kinds of strength we little suspect. We need to undertake voyages of discovery to lay bare the hidden continents of life's possibilities. The recent popularization of such hobbies as painting and sculpture, has startled many of us with the revelation of talent among seemingly ungifted people. In emergencies we have all revealed powers of body and mind of which we were seldom aware. We are all richer than we realize.

Who ever imagined what stupendous energies lay stored up in a single atom of uranium? There are levels of being whose depths we must seek throughout all our lives. He who only lives on the surface enjoys but the outer crust; he who reaches beneath the surface begins to claim his hidden treasures.

Have you ever rebelled because you thought your life was too drab? Dig more deeply. Seek its potentialities. By the alchemy of your probing, your life will often turn from grey to gold.

—*Ben Zion Bokser*

GOODNESS, THE PATH TO GOD

Abraham, in the Jewish tradition, is the man of compassion, sitting at the door of his tent ready to welcome the hungry and needy. On the verse: 'Abraham planted a tamarisk tree (*eshel*) in Beersheva and called there on the name of the Lord, the everlasting God', the Rabbis remark that the initial letters of the word *eshel* represent the Hebrew words for 'eating,' 'drinking' and 'accompanying on the way'. Abraham, say the Rabbis, loved to provide all men with their basic needs irrespective of their way of life. Those he benefitted were generally so impressed that they cast aside their idols to become worshippers of the true God. Religion has all too often suffered severe setbacks because of the repellent quality of some of its representatives. The Abrahamic ideal is that of the religious man of goodwill who brings men to God by his simple goodness.

—Louis Jacobs

WHY ABRAHAM PLANTED A TAMARISK

A familiar rabbinic interpretation of the word "eshel" (tamarisk tree) sees in it an acronym for the three Hebrew words aḥilah, shetia, leenah—food, drink, lodging. This was the rabbinic way of reminding us that Abraham's genuine contribution to the landscape was not simply adding the beauty of a tree, but the nobility of hospitality.

The Vilna Gaon made the brilliant observation that Abraham's purpose in providing these three forms of hospitality was designed to counteract the evils that had been perpetrated in precisely these areas by his predecessors. Adam had sinned through eating, Noah through drinking, and the people of Sodom by denying lodging. In Abraham these transgressions are repaired.

Abraham becomes an inspiration to us to address ourselves to the legacy of evil we have inherited from the past even as we look to him as an inspiration to perpetuate some of the virtues which are part of our Jewish heritage.

—Sidney Greenberg

THE LAUGHTER WHICH HURTS

Torah Reading:
First Day of
Rosh Hashanah

It is told that when Heraclitus and Democritus, two early Greek philosophers, stopped to realize that life was passing them by, Heraclitus wept while Democritus laughed. And the Greek moralist tells us that the laughter of Democritus was more painful than the tears of Heraclitus.

Much can and should be said about the importance of laughter in our lives. Speaking retrospectively, Oliver Wendell Holmes once said, "I might have entered the ministry if certain clergymen I knew had not looked and acted so much like undertakers." Our tradition urges us to serve the Lord with gladness, and gladness means laughter and joy. But as our Sages make clear in their comment on the laughter of Ishmael, not all laughter is constructive and praiseworthy. There is laughter which is vulgar and laughter which is cruel. There is laughter which mocks our dreams and cuts the ground beneath hope. There is the biting laughter which lascerates the timid heart, and wounds sensitive spirits. There is the laughter which leaves permanent scars. There is the hollow laughter of a Democritus which reflects no joy of living but the bitter accents of despair.

Lowell Thomas once reported an experience he had in New Guinea. He was among a group of natives who were viewing their first motion picture. The thing which struck him most about their reaction was that the tribesmen all laughed in the wrong places. When one of the characters on the screen was beaten they burst into laughter. When anyone was killed they simply roared their delight. It occurred to Lowell Thomas through this experience that it is so easy for us to laugh at the wrong times and even to cry over the wrong things.

43

There are many ways of evaluating a human being, and the dimensions of his character. Perhaps a reliable one might be a study of the things which make him laugh, the things which give him joy and bring him satisfaction. Goethe said, "Men show their character in nothing more clearly than by what they consider laughable."

What are you laughing at?

—Sidney Greenberg

GOD, THE KEEPER OF DEPOSITS

In Midrash Rabbah (53:8) Rabbi Adda interprets the word "pakad" as though it were related to the word "pikadon", a deposit. He pictures the Almighty as saying, "I am a keeper of deposits. Amalek deposited with Me a cluster of thorns and so I returned to him a cluster of thorns. Thus it is written (I Samuel 15:2) 'Thus sayeth the Lord of Hosts, I remember what Amalek did to Israel. . . ' Sarah deposited with Me mitzvot and good deeds; therefore I returned to her mitzvot and good deeds."

The sage in the Midrash wanted to reaffirm the enduring quality of goodness. So often we are discouraged by the failure of constructive deeds to bring immediate constructive results. We are frequently equally disheartened by the failure of evil to bring immediate punishment in its wake. Rabbi Adda counsels patience, both in our anticipation of reward for goodness and in our expectation of punishment for acts of wickedness. He reaffirms the doctrine that the mills of the gods grind slowly but they grind exceedingly fine. Robert Louis Stevenson put it this way: "Sooner or later we have to sit down to a banquet of consequences." Ralph Waldo Emerson put the same truth even more emphatically: "The dice of God are always loaded. Every secret is told, every crime is punished, every virtue rewarded, every wrong redressed, in silence and certainty. The thief steals from himself. The swindler swindles himself."

—Sidney Greenberg

WHAT KIND OF LAUGHTER?

Learn to laugh. And most of all, learn to laugh at yourself. The person who can give a riotous account of his own faux pas, will never have to listen to another's embarrassing account of it. He will rarely know the sting of humiliation. He is a delight to be with; but more important, he is enjoying his own life, and applying to his ills and errors the most soothing balm the human spirit has devised—laughter.

—Margaret M. Butts

Laughter should dimple the cheek, not furrow the brow. A jest should be such that all shall be able to join in the laugh which it occasions; but if it bears hard upon one of the company, like the crack of a string, it makes a stop in the music.

—Owen Feltham

Life pays a bonus to those who learn that laughter is a vital part of living. It is one of God's richest gifts. The Lord loves a cheerful giver; but He also loves the cheerful—period. And so does everyone else.

—Edwin Davis.

Religion, in whatever form, is consolation for the pain of life. Humor is the instinct for taking pain playfully. They both are inseparable.

—Max Eastman

The laughter of man is the contentment of God.

—Eugene P. Bertin

A nation that knows how to laugh at itself is stronger and has greater survival value than one that takes itself with ponderous solemnity; the weakness of Germany, since Bismarck's day, lay not in its arms but in its incapacity to make fun of its own institutions.

—Sydney J. Harris

There is the laughter which is born out of the pure joy of living, the spontaneous expression of health and energy—the sweet laughter of the child. This is a gift of God. There is the warm laughter of the kindly soul which heartens the discouraged, gives health to the sick and comfort to the dying. . . There is, above all, the laughter that comes from the eternal joy of creation, the joy of making the world new, the joy of expressing the inner riches of the soul—laughter that triumphs over pain and hardship in the passion for an enduring ideal, the joy of bringing the light of happiness, of truth and beauty into a dark world. This is divine laughter par excellence.

—J. E. Boodin

Laughter is an integral part of life, one that we could ill afford to lose. If I were asked what single quality every human being needs more than any other, I would answer, the ability to laugh at himself. When we see our own grotesqueries, how droll our ambitions are, how comical we are in almost all respects, we automatically become more sane, less self-centered, more humble, more wholesome. To laugh at ourselves we have to stand outside ourselves—and that is an immense benefit. Our puffed-up pride and touchy self-importance vanish; a clean and sweet humility begins to take possessionof us. We are on the way to growing a soul.

—A. Powell Davies   47

The young man who has not wept is a savage, and the old man who will not laugh is a fool.

—George Santayana

Laughter is one of the best things that God has given us, and with hearty laughter neither malice nor indecency can exist.

—Stanley Baldwin

God is the creator of laughter that is good.

—Philo

An ounce of cheerfulness is worth a pound of sadness to serve God with.

—Thomas Fuller

Several parent-child relationships are described in the Torah and Haftarah readings for both days of Rosh Hashanah.

During the last war, London parents shipped as many children as possible into the country where they would be physically safe from air bombardments. Studies made after the war showed that children who remained in London with their parents suffered less, physically and emotionally, than did the children sent to the country for safety. The true security was found to be family unity, not physical safety.

—Henry C. Link

The greatest, most formidable force in the life of a child, with no second competitor, is his home. A leading Eastern university spent a quarter of a million dollars to formally establish this fact. This is approximately how the child's waking time is divided: The public school has him 16% of his time. The church, 1% (if he is consistent in his attendance). The home has him 83% of his time.

—Howard Hendricks

The parent's life is the child's copy-book.

—Author Unknown

One father is more than a hundred schoolmasters.

—George Herbert   49

The great capacity of the Jews and the Chinese, above all other peoples, to survive the cancerous attacks of dehumanized power has derived from their sense of the family; their loyalty to the generations behind them and those yet to come.

—Lewis Mumford

Great ideas and fine principles do not live from generation to generation just because they are good, nor because they have been carefully legislated. Ideals and principles continue from generation to generation only when they are built into the hearts of children as they grow up.

—George Benson

What a father says to his children is not heard by the world, but it will be heard by posterity.

—Jean Paul Richter

God intends that parents, not the children, shall direct the household.

—Arthur S. Maxwell

Parents should live for their children, but not through them; the parents whose satisfactions are wholly reflections of their children's achievements are as much monsters as the parents who neglect their offspring. Nothing can deform a personality so much as the burden of a love that is utterly self-sacrificing.

—Sydney J. Harris

Perhaps parents would enjoy their children more if they stopped to realize that the film of childhood can never be run through for a second showing.

—Evelyn Nown

Torah Reading:
First Day of
Rosh Hashanah

Train children in their youth, and they won't train you in your old age.

—Yiddish Proverb

The child will get a conception of goodness because you are good to him and to other people; of love, because you and your husband increasingly love each other as well as him; of truth, because you are unfailingly truthful; of kindliness of speech, because your words and tones of speech are never harsh; of constancy, because you have kept your promise; of consideration for others, because he sees these things in you.

—A. Fox

A visitor to Coleridge argued strongly against the religious instruction of the young and declared his own determination not to "prejudice" his children in favor of any form of religion, but to allow them at maturity to choose for themselves. The answer of Coleridge was pertinent and sound:

"Why not let the clods choose for themselves between cockleberries and strawberries?"

—Author Unknown

Children have more need of models than of critics.

—Joseph Joubert

51

Children don't want to be told; they want to be shown. It takes years of telling to undo one unwise showing.

—*Ellen M. Haase*

I am the king of a tiny kingdom of three sons. I desire above all things on earth that they may grow up fair and fine and free. Not seldom am I filled with fear of my responsibilities. And because of the knowledge which that fear brings, every day of my life I pray, "God save the king."

—*Studdert Kennedy*

Every child comes with the message that God is not yet discouraged of man.

—*Rabindranath Tagore*

If you can give your children a trust in God they will have one sure way of meeting all the uncertainties of existence.

—*Eleanor Roosevelt*

The *Haftarah* of this day, like the Torah reading, stresses the theme of God's providence over Israel. To enable Israel to survive and fulfil its destiny as a "holy nation," God has always, in crises, raised up leaders who would not merely enable the people to resist their enemies but who would also hold Israel to its covenant with God.

One of the greatest of these leaders was Samuel, the story of whose birth is the subject of this day's *Haftarah*. He lived at the end of the period of the Judges, of whom he was the last, and at the beginning of the monarchy. In that difficult transition from the government of tribal sheiks (Judges), to the national state under the Kings, Samuel was the guiding spirit. His regime terminated the time when "every man did what was right in his own eyes." He unified the people not only politically but also spiritually. His task was recognized by later generations as resembling that of Moses, in bringing all the tribes of Israel into a common convenant with God (see Ps. 99:6). He was also in some respects a forerunner of the Prophets. Like them he taught that to obey God was better than to offer sacrifices to Him.

The prayer ascribed in the Bible to Hannah, the mother of Samuel, sounds the keynote of a theme which recurs frequently in the Rosh Hashanah ritual. God is a righteous Judge by whom "actions are weighed." In the scale in which God weighs human actions, those expressing the will to domination and aggression weigh but little, "for not by force can man prevail."

53

It is significant that this sentiment is put in the mouth of a mother in Israel. The conviction that true success in life is not the result of ruthless self-assertion and aggression, but of honesty, sympathy and kindness, is deeply implanted in our people. That conviction was implanted principally by the mothers of Israel in the hearts of their children. In the midst of a cruel world, in which women of other people incited men to fighting in the gladiatorial combats of the Roman arena, or the jousting fields of the medieval knights, the Jewish mothers taught their children to take pride in being *rahmanim bene rahmanim* (the merciful descendants of merciful ancestors).

—Reconstructionist High Holiday
Prayer Book

THE SIGNATURE OF EVERY MAN

Our prayers deal with the Coronation of God; yet man remains their central theme. Our prayers speak of men and nations; yet man in the singular is their primary target. They recount the annals of universal history, but they do not avoid personal biography as well.

Who are the focal characters of Rosh Hashanah? People! Abraham, Isaac, Sarah, Hagar, Ishmael, Abimelech—these men and women and their problems engage our attention. What are some of the fascinating tales that we read this day out of Scripture? Do we read a tractate on abstract philosophy, or a volume on theoretical ethics, or a folio on principles of society? No! We read about a barren Hannah who longed for a child; about an unhappy Sarah and her domestic problem; about a child dying of thirst in a wilderness, while a helpless mother looked on; about an only son whose father was prepared to offer him upon the altar.

Yes, it is about people that we read. People of flesh and blood! People subject to passion and temptation! People with anxieties and frustrations! People who can stumble and rise again! People who are capable of being a little less than angels and who may be crowned with glory and honour!

On this day, the Jew says to his God, "Thou openest the chronicle of the ages . . . yet the signature of *every* man is in it. . . . A mighty trumpet is sounded, but even a small, still voice is heard." The signature of every man, irrespective of status, of race or of color, must be included in the chronicle of the ages, else it is incomplete. The small, still voice must be heard, else the symphony of life remains unfinished.

55

The importance of man in the singular ought to be readily acknowledged, in particular by our generation. We, more than any other generation, have seen the heights to which man can rise and the depths to which he can sink.

One man brought our world to the brink of destruction. One man threatened to stampede mankind back to the jungle. One man dropped an iron curtain and split the world in two, with terror and hate on one side and fear and suspicion on the other. One man is at this very moment preventing peace in the Middle East and threatening the security of the world. One man snuffed out the life of a young and brilliant president of unlimited promise to his country and the world.

Now, for the other side of the picture. One man and then another called a halt to the dangers and ravages of crippling infantile paralysis. The genius of one man working alone or with colleagues unlocked the secrets of the atom and unleashed power and energy which if constructively harnessed can save the world. One man conceived the formulas and equations which became the Theory of Relativity and enabled us to penetrate the mysteries and vastnesses of outer space.

How true are our prayers! The chronicle of the ages does have the signature of every man in it. And in the din and clamor of life, one can discern the small, still voice even of the most soft-spoken.

—Joseph H. Lookstein

MOTHER LOVE

The problem of the relationship of a mother to her children is a universal one, not only a Jewish one, and it is a profound and troubling one. Erich Fromm in his *Sane Society* has pointed to the deeply tragic character of mother-love. Her dilemma is this: love normally seeks to hold tight, to grow together. In the love between husband and wife, for instance, they may look forward to an ever-growing closeness in the course of the years. Love tends in the direction of unity, reconciliation, increasing closeness. With a child, however, a new element enters. The mother loves the child selflessly and passionately. Without this love, the helpless human child, even more than the animal infant, cannot hope to grow and develop. Yet this love is doomed from the outset, because the mother cannot expect to grow constantly closer to the child as time goes on. She must learn that just as in the early years her intense, holding-type love helped the child *grow*, so she must later withhold this particular expression of love so that he can *grow up*. She must develop in him an independence, to the point where he does not need Mother any more. Mother's very love, which holds tight, must then let go, must help the child *grow away* in order to *grow up*, must help him to achieve emotional independence. Now it is extremely difficult to love and to leave, to hold and to let go, to love passionately when you know that in the end you will not have that which you love. If there is not enough mother-love, there is no growth; if there is too much, there is no growing up, and the child can be permanently infantilized.

Judaism is not unaware of this tragic dimension of mother-love. The Rabbis did not speak of it openly, but they certainly were aware of it and pointed to it in beautiful, symbolic manner.

Hannah, the mother of Samuel the Prophet, is one of the most enduring models of Jewish Motherhood.

She was barren for many years, as were the earlier Matriarchs, and she vowed that when the child was born she would dedicate him to the service of the Temple. Her child Samuel was a frail one, and she kept him with her until he was weaned. Then, while still in his very early youth, she had him sent to the Temple at Shiloh in the care of Eli, the High Priest. Then we read: "Moreover his mother made him a little robe, and brought it to him from year to year when she came up with her husband to offer the yearly sacrifice" (I Samuel 2:19). The Rabbis (in the *Yalkut* to Samuel) tell us that this does not mean that she would bring him a new "little robe" each year, like the mother who knits a sweater for her son away at college. Rather, she made but one "little robe" for him, and she brought it to her son every year, and let him wear it for the duration of the holiday. Then she would take it back with her, and bring it back the year following. And something remarkable happened: although the child grew from year to year, the same "little robe" seemed to grow with him. It always fit; it never was too tight. Samuel became attached to this robe, and even after his mother passed away, he would wear it and he instructed that he be buried in this "little robe," and so it was.

The "little robe" symbolizes mother's love. The robe which gives warmth and embraces the child represents Hannah's love for her Samuel: embracing, warming, attending. Hannah's greatness, however, was that this "little robe" did not stunt Samuel's growth. It grew with her child. Her maternal love was given in such a measure that it conformed to the contours of Samuel's emotional life and needs. As a result, her mother-love never frustrated her child, never smothered him, never infantilized him, even as it never abandoned him. That is why he ultimately asked to be buried in it, because it was permanent and enduring and he wanted it to be with him for all eternity.

—Norman Lamm

THE MOTHERS

Sarah and Hagar are rivals; but they are sisters, too, in their love for their sons and in their anxiety about them. The Haftarah of the first day of Rosh Hashanah associates them with a third sister: Hannah, the childless mother, longing and praying for a son. She cannot even deliver a formulated prayer: "Only her lips moved, but her voice could not be heard," so that the official respresentative of institutionalized religion of those days, Eli, the priest of Shiloh, mistook her for a drunken woman and harshly scolded her. But the day belonged to her: the mother conquered the priest, and we Jews begin every new year with the vivid remembrance of this religious revolution when an inarticulate woman achieved a spiritual grandeur surpassing that of the high priest. In later times its remembrance even became a law, and the Talmud derives the silent Amidah from Hannah's example, (Berahot 31a) thus making the simple, unlearned woman the teacher of the Rabbis.

To close the circle, the Haftarah of the second day, actually following the "binding of Isaac," revives the image of "Rachel, our mother," the archetype of the whole Knesset Yisrael, "bitterly weeping for her children," who are none but the tribes of Israel. In this way the meaning of these chapters moves from the universal level to the specifically national one, coming down from the general human archetypes to the Jewish ones.

—Ernst Simon

ON JUDGING OUR FELLOW MAN

Consider how prone we are to misjudge our fellow-man. All too often we are superficial, impressed by externals, focusing attention upon what a man has rather than what he is. We are like the beggar who approached a kindly-looking gentleman and proceeded to make a moving plea for a contribution. When he had completed his woeful tale, the gentleman said softly: "My friend, I have no money, but I can give you some good advice." The beggar looked at him with contempt. "If you ain't got no money I reckon your advice ain't worth hearing." How many of us use the same reckoning, confusing a man's valuables for his value and his wealth for his worth.

In addition to being superficial in our judgement of others we are too frequently quick to impugn motives and misinterpret deeds. This is a sin from which, as this morning's haftarah testifies, even the greatest are not exempt. We recall how the tormented Hannah came to the temple to pour out her embittered heart before God. She prayed silently, only her lips moving. And Eli, the high priest, misjudges her anguished movements and taunts her: "How long will you remain drunk? Go put away your wine." And Hannah answers, "No, my lord, I am a woman of a sorrowful spirit, I have drunk neither wine nor strong drink, but I poured out my soul before the Lord." Scripture charitably does not record how Eli felt when he heard that soft reply.

A somewhat similar type of incident is described in a modern poem by Rosa Zagnoni Marinoni which may hit a little closer home because it deals with the super-critical motorist. I have often wondered why our most primitive instincts come to the fore when we drive the most modern vehicle. The title of the poem is "Crushed Fender." The poet was driving one night down a narrow street in Milan when she crashed into another car.

I hurled my ire against the guilty one:
"You should be taught to signal as you turn!
At least put out your arm!" I cried at him.
You could have caused our car to overturn!"

At first the man was silent, then he spoke.
"Sorry," he said, "to cause you such alarm.
You did not see it, for the night is dark,
But as I turned, I did put out my arm.

Please take my license number and my name
I hope you will forgive and understand.
I was a soldier once, somewhere in France,
My left arm is a stub. I have no hand."

I could not speak. The words choked in my throat—
I did not take his number, nor his name—
I turned the car against the dull black night,
My face averted to conceal my shame.

Those whom we misjudge do not usually get the opportunity to defend themselves. Would we therefore not do well to pray in the words of the Sioux Indians: "Great Spirit, help me never to judge another until I have walked two weeks in his moccasins." Ought we not to search diligently for the good in others, humbled by the realization that they may have to search even harder to find the good in us? It is this charitable motivation which prompted our sages to say—"Judge not thy fellow-man until thou art in his place." Until we understand his fears and his frustrations, his hopes and his hungers—until we know all that, we ought not to judge for we are too liable to misjudge.

—Sidney Greenberg   *61*

ON JUDGING OTHERS

Eli mistakes Hannah's inaudible prayers for the ramblings of a drunkard. His baseless accusation introduces a theme which touches intimately upon a common human failing.

Oh, great Father, never let me judge another man until I have walked in his moccasins for two weeks.

—Indian Prayer

God himself, sir, does not propose to judge man until the end of his days.

—Samuel Johnson

A man should never be assumed foolish till he has proved himself foolish—this we owe to him. A man should never be assumed wise till he has proved himself wise—this we owe to ourselves.

—Ivan N. Panin

In men whom men condemn as ill
I find so much of goodness still,
In men whom men pronounce divine
I find so much of sin and blot
I do not dare to draw a line
Between the two, where God has not.

—Joaquin Miller

No rewards are offered for finding fault.

—Author Unknown

Only the thinnest line divides the righteous from the self-righteous; the pure from the priggish; the holy from the holier-than-thou; the virtuous from the repressed—and only God knows where the line is drawn.

—Sydney J. Harris

Keep searching for the other fellow's good points. Remember, he has to hunt for yours and maybe he'll be harder put than you are.

—Author Unknown

If we had no faults, we should take less pleasure in noticing those of others.

—Francois Rochefoucauld

Suspicion is far more apt to be wrong than right; oftener unjust than just. It is no friend to virtue, and always an enemy to happiness.

—Hosea Ballou

We must be as courteous to a man as we are to a picture, which we are willing to give the advantage of a good light.

—Ralph Waldo Emerson

Believe me, every man has his secret sorrows, which the world knows not; and oftentimes we call a man cold when he is only sad.

—Henry Wadsworth Longfellow

63

It is literally true that in juding others we trumpet abroad our secret faults. Allow any man to give free vent to his feelings about others, and then you may with perfect safety turn and say, Thou art the man.

—J. A. Hadfield

Rare is the person who can weigh the faults of others without putting his thumb on the scales.

—Byron J. Langenfeld

If it be an evil to judge rashly or untruly of any single man, how much a greater sin it is to condemn a whole people.

—William Penn

How can we venture to judge others when we know so well how ill-equipped they are for judging us?

—Comtesse Diane

I always seek the good that is in people and leave the bad to Him who made mankind and knows how to round off the corners.

—Goethe's Mother

Every man gauges us by himself. A rogue believes all men are rascals; and moral weakness excuses mankind on the same ground. But a Parsival sees no rascality in any one, for the pure see all things purely.

—Author Unknown

SECOND DAY OF ROSH HASHANAH

THE MOUNTAIN FROM WHICH GOD IS SEEN

Torah Reading: Second Day of Rosh Hashanah

The profound and puzzling chapter 22 of Genesis, the story of the binding and near-slaying of Isaac, is the Torah reading for the second day. It is a spell-binding narrative, but its meaning is far from clear. Many modern readers may be reluctant to accept the explanation that God put Abraham through this ordeal in order to test the extent of his unquestioning faith and obedience. Similarly, if the point of the story is to put an end to the custom of human sacrifice, one wonders if this point could not have been communicated to Abraham in a less trying manner.

We may gain a clue to the story's meaning from the repeated use of the word "ra'oh," to see, at critical moments of the narrative. Chapters 21 and 22 of Genesis are part of the *Sidra Vayera* "And God appeared/was seen." In the earlier parts of the Sidra, the issue of seeing and not seeing occurs at several crucial junctures (Abraham and the angels, the blindness of the men of Sodom). In this reading for the second day, Abraham at one point lifts his gaze and sees the mountain of the intended sacrifice from far off. Isaac asks about a lamb, and his father says "God will see to it." After Abraham's hand has been stayed, he sees a ram caught in the thicket. And finally, he names the site of these events *Behar-Adonai-Yeiraeh*, the mountain where God is seen.

What we seem to have here is a story about man's efforts to see God, to find Him and perceive Him as real in the world. Abraham is unique in his generation because he is able to see God at times and in places where others cannot. Could it be that this strange story of the Akedah is the account of how Isaac is taught to see God as his father does? It would then be a form of the coming-of-age-by-ordeal which we

67

know of in many societies, except that what Isaac would have to prove, in order to be accepted as a man, is not physical courage or prowess, but faith and willingness to sacrifice. Perhaps Abraham is saying to his son "I have based my life on dedication to what I believed in, on a willingness to do that which was hard and demanding, and I have found God there. I have found God when I had to do something painful, and I realized that I wasn't alone. And I want you to know that feeling."

It's not enough for Isaac to be Abraham's son. In order to be the continuation of his father's unique heritage, he has to learn to see God in unexpected times and places, because it is that ability that made his father special. He must climb with him up the difficult path to "the mountain from which God is seen."

—Harold Kushner

TAKE YOUR SON

In December 1971, Josef Kramer and his wife presented the main synagogue in Ramat Yosef near Bat Yam in Israel, with a scroll of the Torah in memory of their son. What was so unique about this? What was so important about this that it should have come to light in a book: *"Bizechutam,"* ("Because of Them") written by Yitzchak Nimtsovitz.

The book describes how Josef Kramer built a bunker near his house in a village near Vilna. The Nazis were hunting down Jews in the village, shooting them at sight. A total of forty-seven Jews were concealed in the bunker including Kramer, his wife and their baby son, David.

As the Nazis approached the house, the baby started wailing. All eyes turned to Kramer. The baby was crying. He hesitated for a long, anguished moment and then he strangled his own son with his hands.

And all of the forty-seven Jews in the bunker escaped, some to fight with the partisans, many ultimately reaching Israel.

That was twenty-nine years ago. That's why Josef Kramer and his wife presented the synagogue with a scroll of the Torah in memory of their son, David. That's why present at that ceremony were most of the Jews whose lives were saved by Kramer's desperate sacrifice. And that's why the book was written—to commemorate a sacrifice and to write with a pen dipped into tears the meaning of being part of something, to be attached, to love, to serve, to sacrifice for others.

Could you have done it? Could I? Can we even imagine the enormity of that sacrifice? Was he crazy?

Was he mad? Why did he do it? God, how could he do it? His own child!

He was part of something. He was standing with his people in a bunker, but more than his people, he was standing with his brothers and his sisters attached and bound together by 4,000 years of history and the force of a convenant that commits every Jew to identify with his fellow-Jews and his fellow-human beings—so that the heart of man will never go blind.

—*William B. Silverman*

Of a modern best-seller a critic wrote the cruelest thing you could to it is to read it twice.

Of the story of Abraham and the near-sacrifice of Isaac it may be said that the more you read the more it has to say.

It speaks to us eternally of limitless fidelity and urges us to emulate the father of monotheism in our devotion to godliness.

It speaks to us of God's scorn of human sacrifice. Yes, it is one thing to be willing to give up all; it is another to be the servant of a Deity that wants human beings to exist and not be snuffed out.

It speaks to us of the wholesomeness which comes from, as the story's refrain has it, "father and son walking together." Abraham and Isaac not only walked towards Moriah; they have walked down the corridors of time, beckoning us to create a generation bridge.

It speaks to us of the alacrity with which we should respond to important missions. Abraham's thrice-uttered "Here am I," to God, to his son, and to the Angel is an example to us not to procrastinate when called upon by those who need us.

It speaks to us of the built-in retribution which comes to us when we disregard our loved ones. Just before the near-sacrifice narrative, Abraham treats Ishmael coldly. As a consequence, he must endure what Hagar endured when the son, "whom you love," Isaac, is threatened.

It speaks to us of the sublimity of Abraham's character. When the evil-doers of Sodom and Gomorrah are menaced, Abraham pleads with God on their behalf. When his own son is a seeming target of fate, Abraham does not offer any argument. He reverses, as

71

saints do, the normal priorities. You and I tend to demur when our own people are threatened, and be indifferent to dangers facing strangers. Not so, Abraham, our great model.

The next time you hear the story read, or read it yourself, or think about it, ponder its moral grandeur and then you will understand better what is meant by that segment of the tale which says that Abraham's virtue will result in the uplift and the blessing of "all the families of the earth."

For those who are the descendants of courageous Abraham and intrepid Isaac, the key words here are "noblesse oblige."

—Samuel M. Silver

THE MOST ESSENTIAL LESSON OF LIFE

Rabbi Joseph Hertz, who was chief rabbi of the British Empire, wrote, "The point of the story of the Akedah is that it is a protest against human sacrifice. This is a new era in the history of religion."

Modern Bible scholars such as Sarna and Speiser question this interpretation. They point out that this is really no innovation. Nuzi documents from the age of the Patriarchs prove that animals where being substituted for human beings as sacrifices. Writes Professor Speiser in the new Anchor Bible, *Genesis,* "If it were the intention of the author of Genesis to expose this barbaric custom, then he goes about it in a very strange way." If this were a protest against human sacrifice, would not God have said at the end of the story, "Abraham, offer the ram!" The Bible merely records that a ram appeared. Why is there no moral at the end of the story? If this were a protest against human sacrifice, why not denounce human sacrifice at the end of the episode.

Maimonides, who lived in the twelfth century, explains that God did not doubt Abraham's conviction. God wanted to put Abraham to a pragmatic test, so that Abraham would learn the extent of his own conviction. Did he accept the veracity of the divine call?

Nachmonides believes that it was not a test for the benefit of the tester, meaning God, but a test for the benefit of the tested, meaning Abraham. God knew the outcome in advance.

Sforno explains that Abraham was releasing from his character, qualities of love and awe in emulation of God.

Abarbanel observes that the Hebrew word for "tested," "*Nisa,*" is derived from the word "to lift up." Abraham was lifting up his banner to the world.

73

The answer now becomes more obvious. The entire story is a test of faith. How firm was Abraham's commitment to God? Was Abraham willing to sacrifice for his commitment, even sacrifice his long range objectives?

When God first appeared to Abraham saying, "Leave your father's house," there was a reward implicit in the command, namely that Abraham would become the father of a great people. But now, when He tells Abraham, "Take your son!" no reward is mentioned. Herein is the giant leap. It is the spiritual odyssey of Abraham from the time God first appeared to him until His command to sacrifice his son. Would Abraham heed the call?

God first appeared to Abraham and said, "Lech Lechah," "Will you start out" for the Promised Land? Many of us start out for the Promised land, but encountering obstacles and hardships, we give up. Now comes the end of the odyssey, "Kach Nah," "Are you willing to take your son," to sacrifice everything to reach the Promised Land? Will Abraham maintain his faith even though it appears that everything is lost? Will Abraham perpetuate his ideals even if it entails sacrificing for it?

Abraham, "will you go?" Abraham, "will you give?"

This is not the teleological suspension of the ethical, a leap of faith. A good God does not transcend morality. The reader is forewarned. God never intended that a father sacrifice his child. The test was not to increase God's knowledge but rather to provide a lesson of didactic value to man.

This Biblical story contains the most essential lesson of life. Our lesson is that faith, ideals and goals have meaning only if we are willing to sacrifice for them.

—Hillel Silverman

SUBMISSION TO A HIGHER WILL

Torah Reading: Second Day of Rosh Hashanah

The capacity of Abraham to submit to what he believed to be a higher decree and compulsion is one of the chief traits of mankind at its best. Suffering and sacrifice are not experiences of degradation and self-suppression. On the contrary they ennoble him who practices them and enable him to attain truest self-fulfillment. Self-expression has usually been associated with the idea of giving free rein to one's physical impulses and desires. Equally characteristic of man is the capacity for self-denial in behalf of the person or ideal to whom he is prepared to subordinate himself and his life. To subdue our own wishes by submitting to a higher will is no less a basic human impulse. One of the noble prayers recorded in the Talmud is that recited by Rabbi Eliezer:"Do Thy will O God in heaven above and bestow tranquillity of spirit on those who fear Thee below, *and what is good in Thine own sight do.* Blessed art Thou, O Lord, Who hearest prayer." (Berachot 29b)

No other people has realized to the same degree as Israel that *martyrdom* which is the ultimate in self-sacrifice, when it is practiced for a great cause or ideal is neither defeat nor ignominy. It is triumph, for it marks the victory of man at his best, over his own lower impulses. It is the supreme victory of character over circumstance and intimidation. It is the highest act of faith since it dramatizes the belief in a scale of values in which one's personal welfare, even life, is not the top rung. Never has there been any significant advance in human life, conquest of evil or ignorance except through self-renunciation and sacrifice. Science has its martyrs, and Freedom its heroes of sacrifice no less than Faith.

The classic people of martyrdom has been Israel. Time and again its members unhesitatingly chose

75

death rather than renounce their God and their faith. Martyrdom has a specific name in the Jewish lexicon. It is called "Kiddush Hashem" sanctification of the divine Name. Not only did Israel thus express his supreme devotion to God but also reflected the divine element in human life, which makes it possible for man to put ideals above self. In the early centuries when the decrees of the Emperor Hadrian forbade on penalty of death, the observance of Jewish laws and institutions, so overwhelming was the willingness of people to go to the stake rather than compromise with their conscience, that the Rabbis enumerated three fundamental laws ·with regard to which death should be chosen rather than their violation. These laws were those which prohibited idolatry, incest and murder.

Self-denial is a law of life. Fortunate indeed is he who practices it in behalf of lofty and enduring goals. When Rabbi Akiba, the greatest figure of post-Biblical history, was imprisoned because he violated the Roman decree which forbade instruction of Torah, he found that his fellow-prisoner was Pappus who had doubted the wisdom of risking one's life for such a cause. In prison Pappus turned to Akiba and said, "How blessed art thou Akiba, for thou art confined because of thy devotion to *Torah*, whilst I am imprisoned because of trivial and insignificant acts." (Berachot 61b)

Jewish martyrdom through the ages is not alone a vindication of the Jewish faith, which could breed a race of selfless heroes of the spirit, but likewise evidence of the power of ideals.

—Morris Adler

FOR GOD'S SAKE

In the Talmud (Sanhedrin 86b) one of our Sages, Rabbi Simeon ben Abba, noted that God's order to Abraham is phrased, *"Kah na"* (Gen. 22:2). The word *"na"* means please. In other words, God is pictured as imploring Abraham to meet the test of the Akedah.

This, said the Sage, may be compared to a human king who waged many victorious battles with the assistance of a great general. On the eve of an important battle he turned to his general and said, "I beg you, help me to be victorious in this battle too, lest it be said that my earlier victories were of no consequence." In like manner the Holy One, blessed be He, said to Abraham, "I tested you with many trials and you acquitted yourself honorably. Now meet this trial successfully for My sake, lest it be said that the earlier trials meant nothing."

The thought that emerges from this parable is that God's honor is at stake in Abraham's decision. If Abraham betrays moral inadequacy, God's image is diminished. If Abraham reveals moral fortitude, God's image, as it were, is ennobled.

Here we have a Midrashic comment which elicits the familiar concept of *Kiddush Ha-shem.* God's honor is in man's hands. When we are called to act at our best we should respond not only for our own sake but also for God's sake.

—Sidney Greenberg

THE AKEDAH

The tenth and final trial of Abraham, as described in the Torah reading for the second day of Rosh Hashanah, has been interpreted in many and contradictory ways. It might be considered a "Rohrscharch test," whereby a person's basic bent is revealed. But, no matter how diverse the interpretations, the fantastic power of its imagery was undeniable.

To most commentators, this tale was a reflection of Abraham's unflinching faithfulness. He proved willing to offer not merely his own life, but that of his beloved son. In the famous debate with Rosenstock, Franz Rosenzweig points out that the willingness to sacrifice Isaac, representing the Promise to Abraham, was nobler by far than the self-sacrifice of Jesus in Christian thought. Kierkegaard reflected a persistent theme of Christian Orthodoxy, when he extolled Abraham as "The knight of faith," because he silenced the voice of reason in his own heart and followed the Word of God, even if it seemed absurd.

On the other hand, Jewish philosophers were wont to see the story in the light of the perennial struggle against paganism. In ancient times, the sacrifice of children, especially in times of crisis, was universally regarded as right and proper. The point of the story is the final scene, which foreshadows the prophetic conception of piety. The true sacrifice is a "broken heart." It is what transpires within us that counts, for "the Lord looks to the heart." Judaism emerged upon the arena of history as an impassioned protest against the seductions of popular myths. The false prophets of the unthinking masses have never stopped calling for the sacrifice of children. When theologies lost the mystical power of the "pied piper," ideologies of varied shapes and sizes emerged to serve the same lethal purpose. It is the role of the Jewish people to combat the myths of the masses—myths which bring devastation and death to mankind.

For their pains, our people, like Isaac, live under the perpetual threat of the knife and the fire. Yet, in the nick of time we are saved, and we resume our struggle in the knowledge that it is our destiny to stand for the God of "the still small voice" in the hearts of men and against "the idols of the market place."

—Jacob Agus

THE SUPREME TEST

The Torah reading for this morning describes the familiar, touching story of the supreme test of his faith endured by Father Abraham. He was bidden to take his only son, Isaac, to the top of Mt. Moriah and offer him there as a human sacrifice. Happily, in the nick of time, he was told not to harm a hair on the head of the lad for the God he worshipped did not want human sacrifice. Instead, Abraham sacrificed a ram caught in the thicket in place of his son.

Some phases of the story have not been sufficiently noted by scholars and students. Thus the whole experience is described initially as a *test*. The text begins with the words, "And God *tested* Abraham" for the deliberate purpose of drawing attention to this fact. This was not the case with the other trials Abraham endured. Tradition tells us that "Abraham was tested ten times." But in the other nine instances, there isn't even the shadow of a hint that any one of them was a test. It is the rabbis, many years later, thru the process of retrospective thinking, who speak of Abraham's leaving his father's house, quarrels with Lot, struggle with famine, encounter with Pharaoh, taking up arms to rescue Lot, prolonged childlessness and other harsh experiences, as tests. But here the Bible plainly and very early calls the experience that follows, a *test*.

Then there is something else. Isn't it strange that the father was willing to slay the son without registering a sharp, vigorous protest, especially when the death of Isaac would probably doom his chances of having his own flesh and blood as heir? Look how he argued with God when Sarah was childless, and how he cried out in the agony of his despair. "Of what use are all the blessings You have given me when I am childless?" And how he stormed the very heavèns to save Sodom and Gomorrah, though the inhabitants of the Twin Cities of Destruction were neither kinsmen nor friends of his, except for Lot and his family. Why was Abraham so quiet when the life of his own son was at stake? It is true the rabbis place a demurrer in his mouth, but it is a feeble protest at best.

It seems clear that the answer in both instances is the same. The Bible cautions men against the *excesses* of faith that may result in the cruel fanaticism dramatized so vividly in Arthur Miller's "The Crucible." The emphasis on *test* is to make clear that God never wanted human sacrifice in the first place. Abraham was tested to see how far the faith of this good man would take him, whether he would allow his faith to consume his reason and smother his conscience. When it threatened to do both, he was restrained.

Here is where Soren Kierkegaard, the patron saint of Protestant Existentialism, went astray. In his *Fear and Trembling,* he takes the Akedah as his starting point to construct a system of faith that argues obedience to God as man's ultimate duty regardless of where it leads him. If duty to God requires an act offensive to reason and troubling to conscience, so much the worse for both. When God demands the suspension of the ethical, then let the ethical be suspended. And he uses as his proof, the readiness of Abraham to sacrifice the only son of his old age just because God demanded it.

But a careful reading of the Akedah reveals that the Bible seeks to teach the very opposite. Suspension of the ethical may be good doctrine in other religions; it has no place in Judaism. Indeed, Judaism teaches that man is never nearer to God than when he serves the best interests of his fellows. The whole thrust of the Akedah story is to emphasize that service to God by harming one's fellows is revolting to God.

—Philip Lipis   *81*

TESTING

The Akedah has raised many questions of which I should like to consider only one which is dealt with by the traditional commentators. The Biblical story is introduced by the phrase, *"V'ha-Elohim nisa et Avraham,* God *tested* Abraham."* Since God knows all, it is asked, what need had He for any tests? God certainly knew everything about Abraham including how he would react to the command. How then can we speak of God testing Abraham?

Of all the answers offered to this question the most instructive one is provided by Nachmanides, a medieval Jewish philosopher and Bible commentator. Of course, he says, the omniscient God needed no tests to determine the dimensions of Abraham's devotion. When the Torah says, "God tested Abraham," it is "expressing the situation from the point of view of Abraham." In other words, it was Abraham who looked upon this challenge as a test. He felt that his spiritual mettle was being probed. His character was being plumbed. His stature was being measured.

Nor was this the only time that Abraham felt himself being tested. Tradition teaches us that *"Asarah nisyonot nitnasa Avraham avinu—*Abraham was tested no fewer than ten times."* Again and again when a heavy burden was laid upon him, when a risky assignment was given to him, when a luring temptation was placed before him, Abraham felt himself being tested. Each trial was an opportunity to demonstrate to himself and to his God, the stuff of which he was made.

Is this perhaps the secret of his radiant life? Is this the attitude we need if our lives are to be the meaningful adventures that, especially on Rosh Hashanah, we know they can be? Must we too learn to regard life as a classroom and every experience as a quiz whose purpose it is to determine not what we know but what we are?

Our Sages correctly observed: "There is no creature whom the Holy One, blessed be He, does not test." We are all tested. We are always tested. Whether we are aware of it or not, life is constantly springing little quizzes on us.

The Akedah story has been incorporated into our daily morning prayers, thus subtly reminding us that every day is examination day. As husbands we are tested and as wives we are tested. As children we are tested and as parents we are tested. The doctor confronting his patient is having his dedication tested. The lawyer consulting with his client is having his integrity tested. The rabbi preparing his sermon, the writer at his desk, is each having his honesty tested. The teacher preparing her lesson is having her devotion tested. The businessman on the telephone, the carpenter building a shed, the mechanic under the car, the painter on the scaffold—each is having his character tested.

When a neighbor has been bruised our kindness is tested. When he has been blessed our generosity is tested. When we have been hurt our forgiveness is tested. When we have hurt our humility is tested. Trouble tests our courage. Temptation tests our strength. Friendship tests our loyalty. Failure tests perseverance. Success tests our gratitude.

To look upon life as a test means to bring to it at every time the finest of which we are capable, to keep ourselves always in top moral condition, to realize the enormous possiblilities for good or for ill inherent in each situation regardless of how unspectacular, or humdrum or even ominous it may appear. Ralph Waldo Emerson put this truth in striking words: "It is one of the illusions that the present hour is not the critical, decisive hour. Write it on your heart that every day is the best day of the year. No man has earned anything rightly until he knows that every day is doomsday. Today is a king in disguise . . . Let us not be deceived, let us unmask the king as he passes."

—Sidney Greenberg   *83*

TAKING ALONG ONE'S YOUTH

Abraham took along to the Akedah "two of his servants." The Hebrew words are *Shnay na'arav.* These words, a Hasidic interpretation points out, can also be translated, "The years of his youth." It is worth noting in this regard that according to tradition, Abraham was 137 years old at this time. He could have pleaded infirmity and the disabilities of age as an excuse for not fulfilling the onerous Divine command. But the Bible makes a point of letting us know that despite the anguish and the indescribable heartbreak involved in fulfilling the Divine command, Abraham gathered up his youthful energy and determination in order to fulfill God's word. His zeal not only commands our admiration but also calls for emulation.

—Sidney Greenberg

WHY MOUNT MORIAH?

Two of the most important mountains in Biblical
history are Mount Sinai, the site of the revelation,
and Mount Moriah, on which Abraham bound his son
in fulfillment of the Divine mandate. Many commentators have noted that when the time came for the
Temple to be built, the site chosen was not Sinai but
Moriah despite the impressive case that could be
made for the primacy of the mountain on which the
Israelites accepted the Torah and Commandments.

The choice of Mount Moriah was apparently
designed to remind us that the Temple was to be
linked not primarily with instruction but with deeds
of grandeur and self surrender. Important as it is to
absorb human instruction, it is more important to
perform deeds of valor. Perhaps in some way this
lesson can be linked with the rabbinic aphorism, "Lo
hamidrash ha-ee-kar ela hamaaseh." Not learning but
action is of supreme significance.

—Sidney Greenberg

ABRAHAM'S DOUBLE ACT OF FAITH

When Abraham stayed his hand from slaying Isaac, he shattered a terrifying dogma of his world, and of ours. The ancients practiced the bloody rite of sacrificing their sons, often out of fear that their sons would murder them unless they were done away with first. In our day, we have been taught that the struggle of the fathers and the sons is built into our very natures, that this struggle lies at the heart of all our personal and collective troubles.

Abraham's act teaches us Judaism's belief that this terrifying conflict *can* be overcome. (As a boy I once saw two grown men, a father and a son, savagely beating each other on a street-corner. I will never forget the pain I felt at that scene, and my thinking to myself, "Surely they can't be Jews.") Abraham's act teaches that while we live, nothing in life is so predetermined that it cannot be overcome. Even such a dark event as the generational conflict, rooted in our earliest beginnings, can be transformed by faith into a reconciliation of parents and children. It took the faith of an Abraham, not only to respond to God's first decree to sacrifice Isaac, but to heed the second divine voice, commanding him to spare his son. The second act of faith was even greater because it was man's first revolution against the universal religion which doomed fathers and sons always to be at war with one another.

The war is not over. Only the ancient act of Abraham is proof that it can be ended. Abraham's act is a reminder from the past, and a promise of the future. When, at last, the war of the generations will be ended, it will be accompanied by a truly messianic time. The prophet, Malachi, tells us of the day of the coming of Elijah on which a world shaking event will occur. "He will turn the hearts of the fathers to the children and the hearts of the children to the fathers."

—David Polish

The theme of the *Akedah* story is repeated frequently
in the liturgy of the holiday, both in prose and in
poetic form, and the entire chapter is recited by pious
Jews every morning in their prayers. This manifestation of supreme faith by our father, Abraham, his
readiness to comply with what he believed to be a
divine behest to bring his son, born to him in the
twilight of his life and believed by him to have come
in fulfillment of God's promise, as an offering to the
same God, is invoked by us to avert the severe
judgment that our deeds may merit. We pray that
Providence deal with us in kindness and mercy for the
sake of our ancestors whose devotion and obedience
are so strongly exemplified in the story of the
sacrifice of Isaac. "Abraham mastered his compassion
for his only son in order to perform Thy will with
whole heart; so in like measure may Thy mercy
prevail over Thy stern and strict justice" is the tenor
of the prayer accompanying the recitation of the
story in the liturgy. This is the source for the
theological idea of *Zekhut Abot* (the merit of the
fathers), the appeal made to God to deal mercifully
with us for the sake of the implicit faith and
obedience of the patriarchs, even if we ourselves are
unworthy of considerations of mercy.

Although Abraham did not carry out his intention
to sacrifice Isaac, his good motive should be
accounted as if the act had been accomplished, for
"the merit of good intentions is added to that of
good actions," according to rabbinic teachings.
Abraham's "readiness" to bring his only beloved son
as an offering to God and Isaac's implicit obedience,
so dramatically recorded in the Biblical narrative,
thereby manifesting the suppression of most cher-
ished hopes in behalf of a high ideal, are appealed to

87

as examples of the highest form of piety which should stand in good stead for their children after them throughout all generations. Abraham's intentions were not carried out, but the divine purpose was accomplished—Abraham stood the severe test to which his faith was submitted and that was all that God desired of him.

Besides the lesson which the synagogue derived from the story of the sacrifice of Isaac—the lesson of great faith and unquestioning obedience to the divine will—Bible students regard this narrative as a lesson that God does not desire human sacrifices. The custom of offering children to the deity was prevalent not only among the early Semites, but also among the Egyptians and even among the Greeks and Romans. The tragic story of Iphigenia, the daughter of Agamemnon, who was slain to appease a goddess and whose murder led to a series of assassinations in the family, has been immortalized in Greek drama and has served as a theme also for many a modern poet. Abraham in his great zeal for his newly-discovered faith may have felt that he should do that which was commonly accepted as the expression of the deepest faith—the sacrifice of a beloved child on the altar of the god. The biblical story seeks to stamp out that notion by telling us how Abraham's intention was frustrated by the intervention of God, thus establishing the purer idea that God abhors human sacrifice in any form. Later legislators and seers took their cue from this story and denounced such a form of worship as abhorrent to the God of Israel. This was one of the great moral contributions made to mankind by the Jewish conception of God, at the time when idolatry, even in the most advanced countries of antiquity, still exacted its toll of human sacrifices.

While this may have been the original motive of the story, Jewish tradition is entirely justified in finding *88* in it the noble example of devoted service and complete faith. This act of faith on the part of Abraham and also of Isaac, has served as a stimulus and as a comfort to the large hosts of martyrs through the dark ages when Jews were called upon to sacrifice themselves and their children on the altar of their faith. There is also logic in the fervent prayers of Jews, even at the present time, that this act of Abraham may deter God from imposing upon them the severe penalties that their perversities and sins might ordinarily merit. In prayer and in symbol this thought is emphasized; even the *Shofar* itself, made out of the horn of a ram, is to recall the *"Akedah,"* that great act of faith of our father Abraham, which should act as a *Zekhut* for his children to the end of days.

—Julius H. Greenstone

THREE LEVELS OF MEANING IN THE AKEDAH

"The binding of Isaac" lends itself to three levels of interpretation: the Jewish one, the universal one and the personal one.

On the Jewish level, Isaac became a symbol for those protracted sufferings which have brought our people time and again to the brink of destruction, but not to final ruin. Never was our existence more endangered than in the hour of the Akedah. In the sense of Jewish continuation and continuity Isaac was indeed Abraham's only son. (Gen. 22.2) The whole future of the Jewish people depended on him, and with his premature death we would have been obliterated from the history of mankind. But still the biblical narration of Abraham's. readiness to obey God's terrible command emphasizes his freedom of choice.

He was not forced to do it, he could have resisted it. Physical coercion was not used; only an appeal to Abraham's piety was made; God did not even use the language of command, but that of a request. (Ibid., v.2, cf. Sanhedrin 89b) Therefore, Abraham's willingness was highly praised by God (Ibid., vv. 12,16) and rewarded by the blessing extended not only to him alone, but to his seed after him and through it to "all the nations of the earth." (Ibid., vv. 17,18) This same measure of voluntary sacrifice has been shown by the Jewish people during many chapters of their long history of martyrdom. With the exception of the racial persecutions in our own time, Jews could have escaped their fate, and many in fact did just that. But the remainder behaved with Abraham's stubbornness, Isaac's submissiveness and the religious loyalty of both father and son.

The second level of interpretation, the universal

one, is most easily reached at the moment when the chapter is put into the framework of the readings on Rosh Hashanah. On the first day, we read of Isaac's birth, and of Sarah's jealousy against Hagar and her son. They are sent away into the wilderness. One mother, the Jewess, is now happy; but the other, the Egyptian bond-woman, is most unhappy and prays to God: "Let me not look upon the death of the child." (Ibid., 21.16) Then God "heard the voice of the lad" (Ibid., v.17) and provided him with "a well of water," (Ibid., v.19) thus showing himself as the God of all the peoples, and not only as the God of the Jews.

Abraham was very much grieved about Ishmael, his son with Hagar, before God "tested him" regarding Isaac, his son with Sarah. He went through all the ordeals of a loving father who had to become four score and six years old until his first son was born, and a hundred years old until his second son came. Now he was in danger of losing both of them. In this setting it is the purely "human archetype" of the Father who overshadows all other possible meanings of these Torah readings.

The third level, the personal one, is in this case the most intriguing. How could Abraham believe that God asked from him the sacrifice of his son? Is that a moral demand? And if not, how can it be a religious one? Every generation of simple readers, as well as of sophisticated interpreters, has tried to answer these pertinent questions in its own individual way. There are two main types of answers: a rationalist and a fundamentalist—or today, better put, an "existentialist" one. The rationalists follow a line of thought which may be supported by so early a reaction as that of the prophet Micah,

"Shall I give my first-born for my transgression,
The fruit of my body for the sin of my soul?"
Micah 6:7

91

True, the direct context does not speak here of Abraham and Isaac, but of a general wide-spread custom. It is possible that the prophet hinted at his contemporary, King Ahaz of Judah. (II Kings, 16.3) The Midrash maintains that Micah thought of King Mesha of Moab who offered his eldest son "for a burnt offering upon the wall" and so brought "great wrath upon Israel" which saved him in his deadly predicament (Ibid., 3.27) and of Isaac too (Bereyshit Rabbah 56:6) "Isaac in spite of the fact that nothing was done to him, was accepted as if it had been done, (Cf. ibid., 9.) while Mesha who did his deed, was not accepted." We may go a step further and say: Abraham was accepted because he was asked by God not to do his deed and not to convert "the binding of Isaac" into his "sacrifice." So he made the way free for the sacrifice of animals instead of that of human beings. (Cf. Prof. Shalom Spiegel's excellent paper in Alexander Marx Jubilee Volume, New York, 1950, Hebrew section, pp. 471—547, esp. pp. 29, 33.)

The other school of thought—the "existential"—sees in the absolute submission of Man's will to God's command, even if that seems to be most absurd, Man's highest perfection: in his seeming intellectual degradation he may discover the very height of his spiritual life. According to this view the real victim was not the innocent Isaac, but the knowing Abraham who brought a sacrifice of his intellect and his will, of his emotions and even of his morals, that is, of his whole human personality, *ad maiorem gloriam Dei.*

Between these two extreme positions—the rationalist and the existential—some intermediate possibilities exist, not necessarily of a compromising nature, but authentic in themselves. Our chapter may serve as a warning against a simple identification of religion and ethics. While both of them have their own realm, they are not interchangeable. Nevertheless they are certainly closely related to one another.

Judaism is an ethical religion. It is neither a secular system of morals nor a blind devotion to a supernatural power which may be Satan as well as God. The same Abraham who was ready to sacrifice his own son, was not ready to see the heathen and wicked towns of Sodom and Gomorrah destroyed and fought with God for their survival. He even dared to remind God of his unchangeable ethical character without which he would not be God, and cried to him: "That be far from Thee to do after this manner, to slay the righteous with the wicked, that so the righteous should be as the wicked; that be far from Thee; shall not the Judge of all the earth do justly?" (Gen. 18.25) The partners of this dispute are identical with the partners of the *Akedah*, but an undeniable tension exists between Chapters 18 and 22, in which those two stories are related. It is the tension between "ethics" and "religion" so characteristic for an ethical religion which never eliminates one of its constituent elements for the benefit of the other. In case that there is a real contradiction between our ethical convictions and what is proclaimed as God's will, we should renounce the voice of our conscience only in the extreme case that God's voice speaks to us with the same distinctiveness as it spoke to Abraham (Buber). Further: that was not the case when others would be the victims (Sodom and Gomorrah), but only when he himself was summoned to bring the highest sacrifice. However, if the slightest possibility of an illusion does exist, we should follow our own ethical convictions.

It should be added, that the Akedah is the great exception and not the rule. The rule in Judaism is that religious and moral commands are very close to each other. Therefore, on the one hand, we cannot make atonement to God on Yom Kippur before we have tried to make atonement to our neighbor against whom we have sinned, which emphasizes the moral point, and therefore, on the other side, David could say in his Psalm of repentance on the murder of Uriah "Against Thee, Thee only, have I sinned," which emphasizes the religious point: without the existence of God there would be no sin.

All sins of man against his fellow-men are sins against God, too, but not all sins against God are sins against men. As we have said: ethics and religion are close to each other, but not identical.

—Ernst Simon

CHILD SACRIFICE

In Biblical religion, the practice of child sacrifice is condemned as an affront to the sanctity of God's name (Lev. 20:1-5). The offering of the first-born as a sacrifice, a widespread practice in primitive religion, is in the Torah transformed into the rite of the redemption of the first-born, to serve as a reminder of the intervention of God in the redemption of Israel from Egyptian bondage (Exod. 13:12-15). It took centuries to uproot the pagan practice of human sacrifice. Ahaz, king of Judah "made his son to pass through the fire, according to the abominations of the heathen, whom the Lord cast out from before the children of Israel" (II Kings 16:3). King Manasseh did likewise (II Kings 21:6). Child sacrifice is also reported to have been practiced in the Northern Kingdom of Israel (II Kings 17:17). A grim reminder of this practice is the word *gehenna* derived from *Ge ben-Hinnom* (the Valley of ben-Hinnom) to the Southwest of Jerusalem, where an altar had been erected to the idol Moloch to whom children were sacrificed (II Kings 23:10). That the God of Israel reviled human sacrifice and counselled a different way to serve Him is expressed with eloquence by Micah:

> "Wherewith shall I come before the Lord . . .
> Shall I give my first-born for my transgression,
> The fruit of my body for the sin of my soul?
> It hath been told thee, O man, what is good,
> And what the Lord doth require of thee:
> Only to do justly, and to love mercy, and to
>   walk humbly with thy God."
>
> Micah 6:6, 8

It was in rabbinic times, when child sacrifice was no longer practiced even among the pagan neighbors of Israel, that the theme of the *Akedah* proved to be particularly significant. Out of a sense of utter humility before God, a contrast was drawn between the self-sacrificing devotion of Abraham and Isaac, and the inconstancy of the faith and practice of the average person. It was from this impulse that the doctrine of *Zekhut Avot* (Merit of the Fathers) was developed to encourage the people in the expectation that their prayers would be heard in spite of their deficiency. The doctrine avowed that while the descendants of Abraham and Isaac may have fallen far short of what God demands of them, they can invoke His mercy and secure His forgiveness because of the "merit" established for them by Abraham and Isaac in having met the test of the *Akedah.* Indeed, the *Akedah* is so dominant a theme in the liturgy of Rosh Hashanah that Rabbi Abbahu makes the observation that when, on Rosh Hashanah, we blow the ram's horn, reminiscent of the ram that Abraham used as a substitute for Isaac (Gen. 22:13), God accounts it as if each worshiper had actually bound himself on the altar as a willing martyr to God (R.H. 16a).

—Max Arzt

ON TELLING THE AKEDAH TO CHILDREN

I am becoming more and more convinced that we have failed as parents and grandparents because we did not allow our children often enough to be without that which they craved. Moreover I would want them to know that this denial is because they are Jewish. Of course it is important to have them feel their lives are enriched because they are Jewish but equally important is the knowledge that because they are Jewish they cannot have everything. They must sacrifice. They must even suffer.

Not too long ago I raised a very important question with my congregation. Indeed it was suggested by one of our members. Is it right to teach children about a God who wants Abraham to sacrifice his favorite son upon an altar to prove his devotion? What kind of a God is that? What kind of compassion does He have?

Recently this topic was discussed by a Christian woman who never wanted to hear the story of the binding of Isaac because she felt the story was so inhuman that it made her sick every time she heard it. She finally discovered after very careful self-analysis that she loathed the story because when she was a child she suffered from a very severe illness which required long surgery and she had the most vivid recollection of her father delivering her to the hospital to men in white who performed the surgery giving her only a local anaesthesia. This horrible memory she always associated with Abraham placing his son upon the altar. She then understood why she never wanted to hear the story.

However, my problem was that this question has never been raised by Jews before. Why is it that in thousands of years of pondering the subject no one questioned the wisdom of narrating the story unto children?

97

It occurred to me that the reason this question did not bother Jews or antiquity was that they saw nothing wrong in having children understand from their earliest childhood that to live Jewishly means to sacrifice; to live Jewishly means to be prepared to do without.

I am becoming more and more convinced that it is important for Jewish children not to be sheltered. Perhaps that is why they are not prepared for Jewish living when they grow up. Perhaps that is why they are incapable of assuming leadership in the Jewish community even though they say they want it. They are simply unprepared for the sacrifices that leadership involves.

Even sacrificial giving is more often made manifest by Jewish adults than by Jewish youth. This is the consequence of our having been so careful for so long to see to it that our children had everything and were denied nothing.

—Emanuel Rackman

NOT TRAPPED, BUT TESTED

One interpretation of life, which western civilization has inherited from ancient Greek culture, is that human life is the inevitable working out of a dire doom from which there is no escape. Man may delude himself with the belief that he is free to make of his life what he will, but in actuality he is trapped by a destiny which is deaf to his most heart-rending appeals. The very antithesis of that is the version of life implied in the Jewish religion. According to that version, human life is part of the process of creation which God initiated, a process in which the future always somehow redeems the past, and man is always being tested as to how long he can hold out in awaiting that future.

The idea of Fate, or Necessity, which in one form or another is to be found in every civilization, became a veritable obsession with the Greeks. It attained a depth and pathos unknown to any other people. It is writ large on almost every page of their great literature. . . . Euripides put it clearly in *Orestes:*

> "Ye tear-drowned toiling tribes
> Whose life is but a span,
> Behold how fate, or soon or late,
> upsets the hopes of man!
> In sorrow still your changing state
> Must end as it began."

The pattern of the world as the ancient Greeks conceived it may be said to have been that of a huge spiderweb, at the center of which Fate, or Necessity, like a great spider, feeds on the victims caught in the filaments of the web. In his ignorance man worships these very filaments as gods, praying to them to help

99

him in his struggle against Fate, forgetting that they themselves are nothing but the very ooze of Fate. "Ah me! if Fate, ordained of old, held not the will of gods, constrained, controlled," sings the Chorus in Aeschylus' *Agamemnon.* "Pray not at all, since there is no release for mortals from predestined calamity," says the Chorus in Sophocles' *Antigone. . . .*

According to the version which the Jewish civilization at its best has always given to man's place in the world, life is conceived not as the working out of a doom but as the fulfillment of a blessing. The process of that fulfillment is continually interrupted by all manner of evil. Evil is an interference; it is not Fate. "The die is cast," says the occidental man; and Jewish religion retorts, "But the final issue is with God." For God is the creator, and that which seems impossible today He may bring to birth tomorrow.

Once we learn to regard evil as the chance invasion of sheer purposelessness, and learn to identify all meaningful factors in the world with good and blessing, we become adjusted to whatever befalls us, not in the spirit of desperate resignation, but of hopeful waiting. Thus, for example, the Jews have been taught to regard their national history in the light of the blessing which God had bestowed upon Abraham. Though every page of that history records unparalleled suffering and tragedy, the Jews as a people never for one moment surrendered their faith in the blessing. The suffering and the tragedy have always been viewed merely as interruptions which have postponed the fulfillment of the blessing. They were never thought of as the fulfillment of some irrevocable doom. It is only Christianity, which has assimilated a great deal of the Greek spirit, that has made the doctrine of original sin a fundamental teaching. Calvinism, with its crystallization of Jewish thought into the fixed molds of western logic, has gone so far as to make of God a cosmic monster who delights in the tortures of the eternally damned.

According to Jewish traditional teaching, man is not trapped but tested. His vicissitudes should serve as a challenge to his faith, and patience in the face of the retardation of that blessing which he has a right to expect with the gift of life. To deny the worth of life and to fall into despair because the promise is slow of fulfillment is to fail in the test. This is the main point in the cycle of Abraham stories, which culminates in the account of the test to which God put Abraham when He commanded him to offer up Isaac.

Torah Reading: Second Day of Rosh Hashanah

—Mordecai M. Kaplan

JEWS ON EASY TERMS

Through ourselves we Jews, like every other people, can reach the world. But we must remember that the affirmative powers in us and their interplay with the world situation, call for the acceptance of a heavy discipline. Only the terrific illusion that we can be Jews on easy terms, that we can take life as it comes, tacitly—as others do—can be fatal to us. In childhood and manhood we must carry the yoke which our forebears carried, and we must carry it gladly, because the only alternative is an intellectual and moral leprosy from which there is no escape unto death.

—Maurice Samuel

TORN BETWEEN TWO LOVES

The moral problem on which the Abraham and Isaac story sheds light is the problem of a soul torn between two strong attachments. Abraham loved God with all his heart and soul. Abraham also loved his son. Suddenly the two loves are brought into clash. Abraham is ordered to sacrifice his son to prove his devotion to the Creator of the universe. And what was Abraham to do? Should he foreswear God or should he surrender his beloved offspring? You can readily visualize the turmoil in his soul. Yet Abraham promptly concluded that he must slaughter his son. Why? Why didn't he argue with God? Arguing with God was nothing unusual for Abraham. He had argued with God when God was about to destroy the cities of Sodom and Gomorrah. He had argued with God when on an earlier occasion God had made what appeared to be an empty promise. Why, then, didn't he argue with God when God ordered the sacrifice of his son? And a good argument he had—as the Midrash observes. He could have told God that it was God Himself who had given the assurance that through Isaac, Abraham's descendants would fill the earth. How, therefore, could God now order Isaac's death? But Abraham said nothing. He reasoned, one presumes, that he had no choice. After all, as against an individual son, who is only a tiny speck of humanity, one must of necessity prefer God, who is universal and all-embracing; as against a private interest—one's own flesh and blood—one must of necessity prefer God who is the totality of all of nature and more.

But lo and behold, while Abraham thought he had chosen wisely, God intervened at the crucial moment to save Isaac and teach Abraham a great moral truth. Though Abraham had proven how devoted he was to God, God commanded him, "Do not touch the lad."

God may be the greater and more universal Object to be loved but that is not necessarily a reason for suppressing a father's natural love for his child. On the other hand, because of one's great love for the omnipresent Almighty, one's love for one's near and dear ought be greater than ever. And if the two loves sometimes seem to conflict with each other perhaps it is because we do not correctly comprehend what is our true obligation to each. That is why our sages tell us that Abraham really misunderstood God's command. Had he argued with God, perhaps he would have discovered God's real will. But he should not have blithely assumed that God wanted Isaac's death. The truth is that the proper love of one's near and dear is the means by which one achieves the deepest love of God. Love of individuals is the anchor from which one probes to discover and fulfill even more universal loves.

—Emanuel Rackman

HEARTS BOUND WITH LOVE

God,
We cannot comprehend
What You asked of Abraham:

> "Take your son,
> Your only one, whom you love—
> Isaac. . . .
> And offer him up as a sacrifice."

We are the children of Abraham,
Believing what we cannot comprehend:

> We believe You require human sacrifice—
> Not of bodies bound with ropes,
> But of hearts bound with love.

We believe our sacrifice is dear to You,
That the gift of our hearts builds the world.

> We believe that what we say matters to You,
> That our words vanishing into the wind
> Echo forever.

We believe our deeds matter,
That in Your sight
Our daily trifles rival in importance
The awesome galaxies

> We believe that what we do today—
> Baring our hearts before You,
> Seeking Your presence,
> Calling Your name—
> Is the reason You created us.

We believe You remember those two fragile forms:
Isaac's young body on the altar
And his father, bowed with years,
Who did not flinch before Your will.

We believe that the faith of those two mortals
Long ago, unobserved by other eyes than Yours,
Is the fabric of our lives.

Though imprisoned in our mortal frames,
We, like them, can do Your will—
Every day of our lives.

We believe You require human sacrifice—
Not of bodies bound with ropes,
But of hearts bound with love.

—Michael Hecht

BELIEVING GOD

Emunah is more than just agreement that a certain proposition is logically true. One does not believe in God in the same way that one believes in proportional representation, or socialized medicine or the practicality of the monorail. *Emunah* is faithfulness. It is the willingness to trust oneself to God and to live all of one's days within His Presence. As one writer has put it: "The man of faith does not believe in the idea of God. He believes God!"

To believe in the logical idea that there is a God costs very little. To believe God involves and requires the believer's entire life. Franz Rosenzweig has explained the difference between opinion and faith in these words:

"From those unimportant truths of the type of 'two plus two equals four', to which men lightly assent with the expenditure of no more than a trifle mind energy—a little less for the multiplication table, a little more for the theory of relativity—the way leads up to those truths for which a man is willing to pay something, and then on to those that he cannot prove true except by the sacrifice of life."

—Author Unknown

ABRAHAM AND ISAAC

Abraham:

    I dreamed that my first-born of Sara
    would be the father of a great nation,
    a nation as numerous as the sands of the sea,
    as bright as the stars of heaven.
    I taught him to be a chieftain
    but I forgot that God demands of us our
    first-born.
    It is easier when they are infants,
    but now I know the lad, slender and quick;
    he leans against me and my hand rests on his
    curly head.
    How can I do what I must do?
    Oh my God! I would give back every promise
      Thou hast made me
    for the life of my son, my only son, Isaac!

Isaac:

    My father led me up the mountain,
    tied me down on the uneven faggots
    with my head thrown back.
    I saw his hand, the knuckles white,
    clutching the knife with the jagged edge:
    I knew that when my throat was cut
    and my blood running out on the ground
    death might not come before the burning.
    But then my father's hand stopped in mid-air,
    and I heard the angry bleating of the ram.

Abraham:

    Oh God, I know Thee now,
    not as a maker of covenants,
    but as the giver of life.
    I pray to Thee:
    Let my son dream his own dreams, not mine.   *107*

Let him make his own promises to Thee.
Let him live the life Thou hast bestowed upon
  him
as Thou and he see fit.

Isaac:
My father used to teach me many things
so I could learn to be a great chieftain,
but since we went up on the mountain
he is quiet and gentle and only tells me
that as I grow older I, too, will speak with God.
When I wander in the fields at eventide
and sometimes watch a caravan pass by
I think about my father finding the ram
and I wonder what God will require of me.

—Ruth F. Brin

A number of commentators, including the Kotzker Rebbe, point out the significance of the fact that Abraham does not actually reach the mountain on which the Akedah is performed until a lapse of three days. His willingness to honor his commitment after an interval of several days is especially worthy of note and emulation.

All too familiar is the initial burst of enthusiasm in response to a profound emotional appeal or stimulus. We witness it on the High Holy Days when all kinds of lofty resolves well up within us. But what happens on the third day? What happens when the spell is broken and the memory of the synagogue recedes into the background? Are we still as determined to honor our commitments and redeem our promises to ourselves and to God? A true test of our zeal is not the immediate response—"And Abraham rose up early in the morning." The true measure of his spiritual stamina was revealed on the third day.

The Midrash in commenting on this verse quotes Hosea (6:2) "He will revive us for two days and on the third day He will establish us and we shall live before Him."

—Sidney Greenberg

HE SAW THE PLACE FROM AFAR

Everyone who has dealt with children knows the youngster who sits down to eat a meal and wants to consume the dessert first. It takes persuasion, or, more frequently, a display of authority to bring the child to understand that it must learn to postpone the delights of the cake or ice cream until after the meal has been eaten.

This characteristic of children's behavior is not confined to them nor is it limited to the dinner table. There is noticeable among many teenagers and adults in our time the tendency to grasp the things which are immediately present without any thought of the future.

A large number of the baneful pleasures of young people is directed to deriving a momentary thrill from something whose long-range consequences are anything but good. Even in such an important matter like the choice of a husband or wife, how many are there who ask themselves what sort of father or mother the other person will be? Most young people think only in terms of some temporary infatuation, of a charm which quickly disappears.

There are, among others, two well-known defects in human vision. One is myopia, or what is better known as near-sightedness, while the other is presbyopia or far-sightedness. The former describes the ability to see what is close at hand and the inability to see things at a distance. The latter is the ability to see what is far off but an inability to see what is close at hand.

Young people, mostly, suffer from myopia i.e. they can see what is close by but cannot discern what is removed either in space or time. Older people usually are afflicted with presbyopia (derived from the Greek word for "old"), and can behold the distant vista but cannot read the numbers in the telephone book.

In the Torah reading of Rosh Hashanah, there is a description of Abraham's journey to the mountain with his son Isaac. As he traveled, we are told, "he saw the place from afar." I am not so sure that the son saw the distant view because he was probably concerned with what was in his immediate surroundings.

We need spiritual oculists who will teach the old to see what is near and make them realize that one cannot defer joys to an uncertain future. But I think it more important to overcome the myopia of youth and to point to distant goals.

—Harry Halpern

BRIDGING THE GENERATION GAP

Genesis 22:8

Everyone under the sun is trying to understand the generation gap. One Dr. Baumrind, a psychologist, tells us that the excesses of youth in our generation is encouraged by two types of parents: one, authoritarian, the other, permissive. The authoritarian parent controls the behavior of his child in accordance with absolute standards. There is no give and take and the child must submit to adult rule simply because it is adult. No wonder the child rebels in his adolescence. He busts out because he is violently reacting to his being deprived of opportunities for independent action.

The permissive parent functions on the other side of the scale. He disdains controls; he strives to permit his child to freely express himself without any parental interference. Studies show that this non-interference tells the child that his way is always justifiable. And so when this youngster grows to adolescence he is convinced that no institution can possibly tell him what to do. He goes on his merry, independent path, thumbing his nose up at authority when it gets in his way.

The good guy in this story is the third type of parent, the authoritative parent. This parent tries to understand a child's hungering for independence but also sets standards for conduct and achievement. The rules and regulations this parent sets is not projected through absolute authority but in a rational manner that encourages discussion. The youngster grows up independent of thought but understanding of the role of authority in society.

The generation gap rebels come from the first two groups, says the doctor. Some of us parents who thought we belonged to the club of authoritative parents, the good guys, wonder why this theory doesn't always seem to work.

We have to have these qualities in dealing with college students: "*One*. The power to listen, not just to hear. *Two*. The capacity to counsel, not just direct. *Three*. The need to respect and affirm the dignity of the student, not to treat him as a kid. *Four*. To call him to high tasks and not just to criticize low achievements. *Five*. To cultivate a sense of involved partnership rather than adult-child, rabbi-congregant confrontation. *Six*. To cultivate idealism and moral sensitivity, not just insitutional obedience and survivalistic loyalty."

—Philip Arian

WHY OUR CHILDREN DON'T TRUST US

Stekel, that brilliant and erratic psychiatrist, said near the end of his life: "When I look back upon the long series of nervous diseases that I have observed, I see that invariably the parents have failed to practice what they preached to their children."

This comment, more than anything else, seems to me to sum up the chief reason for the resentment, the restlessness, the rebellion of so many American youths today. We are living in a culture which shows all the symptoms of a split personality. And our children do not know which part of us to believe, to trust, to follow.

On the one hand, we preach the Judeo-Christian system of ethics: to treat our fellow men decently, to extend mercy, to behave with honor, to place the welfare of our community above our own solf-interest.

On the other hand, we secretly (and sometimes openly) respect the qualities of cunning, shrewdness, self-seeking, duplicity, and the aggressive accumulation of material goods.

On Sundays we worship the God of our fathers; on weekdays we make supplication before the idols of the market place. We send our children to Sunday school in the morning; and in the afternoon we bribe a policeman to refrain from giving us a ticket for speeding.

Children take in more with their eyes than with their ears. They recognize that our homilies about honesty do not always jibe with our personal practices, at home, in the office, or on the road.

If we tell them to value the quality of "sharing," and then we boast about our "sharp deal," they intuitively know that we are not handling our lives the way we tell them to handle their toys.

What Erik Erikson in his magnificent book *Child-hood and Society* calls "basic trust" is the most important legacy we can leave a child. But when the child cannot trust us, when he witnesses the gross disparity between our preachments and our practices, then he feels baffled and cheated, and runs wild because he has no guidelines he can cling to.

When parents talk about "discipline," they mean a rigid set of rules to prevent the child from mis-behaving. But the only discipline worthy of the name lies in providing a solid framework of ideals—not for the child to live up to, but for the parents to live within.

You can beat a child until he is black and you are blue, but it cannot make him any better than the examples he sees around him every day.

—Sydney J. Harris

THEY BOTH WENT TOGETHER

One of the most interesting people I met in Moscow was a middle-aged man who several years ago went to the synagogue for the first time since his childhood; since then he has regularly returned for the High Holy Days. There was no religious motivation; he simply wanted to see Jews, he felt comfortable, at ease, among them. He told me about himself.

He was a professor at the university, a soldier in the Second World War, from which he had returned with an impressive number of decorations. Even though his father had been an active Communist, the fact that he was Jewish was a great liability to his career at the university. Had he been Ukrainian or Uzbek he long ago would have occupied the position which he deserved, appropriate to his experience and ability.

One day he came to the conclusion that since, regardless of the Slavic name he had adopted and his non-Jewish wife and his party card, he would always be considered a Jew, he might as well have some benefits from being a Jew. Therefore, two or three years ago, he went to watch the young people dance on Simhat Torah. Suddenly, while watching them sing and dance in the street in front of the synagogue, he was overcome by an extraordinary sensation. One face in the crowd seemed familiar to him. He jumped up and embraced a young man in a komsomol uniform. "It was my son," he told me. "I did not know that he came there, just as he did not know that I came." The boy, who was sixteen years old, told his father that he had started going to the synagogue on Simhat Torah, but never spoke of it to his father for fear of embarrassing him. Like the father, the boy did not know why he came; just that he felt good being with these girls and boys.

—Elie Wiesel

WHAT DO YOU SEE?

Emerson has written: "That only which we have within can we see without. If we meet no gods it is because we harbor none. If there is grandeur in you, you will find grandeur in porters and sweeps."

What we see in life is a reflection of our own inner selves, what we bring to it. The gossip condemns himself. Those who always find meanness in others have meanness in themselves. Those who constantly find goodness in others have goodness in themselves. How the world looks to us depends upon how we look at it, the perspective we bring. There is as much truth as humor in the observation that "whether or not it's bad luck to meet a black cat depends on whether you're a man or a mouse."

If we bring friendship we will receive friendship. Kindness evokes kindness.

An anonymous poet has put this truth into a poem which compensates with accuracy what it lacks in sophistication.

> "It's a gay old world when you're gay
> And a glad old world when you're glad;
> But whether you play
> Or go toiling away
> It's a sad old world when you're sad.
>
> It's a grand old world if you're great
> And a mean old world if you're small;
> It's a world full of hate
> For the foolish who prate
> Of the uselessness of it all.

It's a beautiful world to see
Or it's dismal in every zone
The thing it must be
In its gloom or its glee
Depends on yourself alone."

—Sidney Greenberg

WHAT DO YOU SEE?

Three men looked at the spectacular Grand Canyon. The first was an archeologist who exclaimed: "What a wonder of science!" The second was a clergyman who whispered: "One of God's great glories." The third man was a cowboy whose laconic comment was: "A heck of a place to lose a cow."

—Sidney Greenberg

WHAT DO YOU SEE?

Our Sages tell us that as Abraham and Isaac and their servants approached Mount Moriah, the divinely designated summit for the sacrifice, Abraham turned to his servants with a question: "Do you see anything in the distance?" They stared and shook their heads. "No, we see only the trackless wastes of the wilderness." Abraham then turned to Isaac with the very same question. "Yes," said the son, "I see a mountain, majestic and beautiful, and a cloud of glory hovers above it." It was at this point that Abraham directed his servants to remain behind while he and Isaac continued on their mission alone.

Here then is our text for this day. Two people facing in the same direction, surveying the identical scene, come up with completely different impressions. One sees only emptiness and barrenness ahead. The second sees the majestic and challenging mountains. The difference obviously lay in the eyes of the beholder.

Skipping the centuries now and coming right here into the synagogue, let us each ask ourselves the question—"What do you see?" As we shall soon realize, this can be a decisive question.

On this day when we pray for life, we might, therefore, each ask ourselves-what do you see in life?

When you look at your life, do you habitually see reasons for grumbling or gratefulness? Do you feel that you have been short-changed or over-paid? Do you constantly feel your cup is half empty or in the words of the psalmist, "my cup runneth over"?

Matthew Arnold has written that "one thing only has been lent to youth and age in common—it is discontent." Our favorite posture is one of protest and we who have so much, so very, very much, often permit the one thing we lack to blind us to the great wealth we possess.

119

When you look at life, do you see only your life and your needs, or do you see the lives and the needs of others as well? Do you see life as a campaign of acquisition or as an adventure in sharing? This question is basic because it spills over into every area of life. How do you regard your job or profession? Is it only a means of providing you and your family with your needs and luxuries, or is it also an opportunity to render a service? How do you regard your mate in marriage? Someone created for your comfort and convenience or someone whose life you can enrich and ennoble? How do you regard your fellowman? Someone whose main function in life is to serve as a stepping-stone to your success or someone with hopes and needs just like yourself?

When you look at life, do you look with fear or with faith?

It is impossible, of course, to be entirely free of fear. There is literally no one without his share of fears and apprehensions. The bravest of men have a fear of losing loved ones, a fear of losing health and fortune. To a certain extent, of course, our fears are the saving of us. The man who fears failure develops his skills and his talents more fully. The fear of separation from loved ones spurs us on in medical and scientific research and "the beginning of wisdom," the psalmist tells us, "is fear of the Lord." But fear becomes a matter of deep concern when it becomes exaggerated and morbid, when instead of leading to action it creates a paralysis of will, when it succumbs to the very object of its dread.

Beginning with the month of Elul and continuing through Hoshana Rabba, we add Psalm 27 to our daily Service. That Psalm might well be our watch-word not only for these days but throughout the year.

"The Lord is my light and my salvation, whom shall I fear? The Lord is the fortress of my life of whom shall I be afraid?"

The cardinal irreverence in Judaism is to be afraid of life, for when we fear life we betray a lack of faith in God. Faith in God does not mean to believe that sorrow will never invade our homes, or illness never strike us and our loved ones. Many people who cherish such a naive belief are due for heart-breaking disillusionment. It is these people who will say to you: "When my mother died, I stopped believing in God." They believed the wrong things about God to begin with. To believe in God is to have faith that He will give us, admist all vicissitudes, the strength to endure, and the power to hold on and see it through, the capacity to translate even our trials and our tribulations into moral and spiritual victories.

What do you see in life—the parched desert of fear or the inspiring mountain of faith?

—Sidney Greenberg

IF THE ANGEL HAD BEEN LATE

Here is the experience of a child of seven who was reading in school the chapter which tells of the sacrifice of Isaac:

> Isaac was on the way to Mount Moriah with his father; then he lay on the altar, bound, waiting to be sacrificed. My heart began to beat even faster; it actually sobbed with pity for Isaac. Behold, Abraham now lifted the knife. And now my heart froze within me with fright. Suddenly, the voice of the angel was heard: "Abraham, lay not your hand upon the lad, for now I know that you fear God." And here I broke out in tears and wept aloud. "Why are you crying," asked the rabbi. "You know that Isaac was not killed."
>
> And I said to him, still weeping, "But, rabbi, suppose the angel had come a second too late?"
>
> The rabbi comforted me and calmed me by telling me that an angel cannot come late.

An angel cannot be late, but man, made of flesh and blood, may be.

—*Abraham J. Heschel*

The inspiration which the "Akedah" has given to Jews throughout the generations rests upon the assumption that Isaac was indeed sacrificed, whereas the whole point of the story is that he was *not* sacrificed! The dramatic element is provided by the contrast between the willingness of Abraham to offer up his son and the unwillingness of God to accept that offering, and this contrast gives a new meaning to the words of the angel. I hear him saying in a gentle, chiding voice: "I desire only the will but not the deed. It is in the spiritual and not the physical, surrender to God that lies the true sign of the servant of God. I do not ask that the Jew should *die* as a Jew, but that he should *live* as a Jew. Is not the whole purpose of the Jew in the world that he shall bring a blessing to mankind?" "And through thee shall all the nations of the earth be blessed." It is not by dying for Judaism, but by living for Judaism that that ideal will be fulfilled!

To live as a Jew! Is there a better phrase in which to sum up in a few words the whole burden of our prayers on this day, what we ask of God, and what in return God asks of us, than the phrase to live as a Jew? For what is it that we ask of God? Like the clang of a hammer on a plate of brass, the reverberating of "Zochrenu l'Chaim" ("Remember us, O Lord, for life") resounds throughout our whole prayers. Inscribe us for a good life; take us not hence in the midst of our days. Grant that we may enjoy life, for "the dead shall not praise God." And what is it that God demands from us in return for that boon of life? That we live as Jews, proud and conscious of our responsibilities to Him and to ourselves.

—Louis Rabinowitz

123

THE ELEVENTH TEST

In the hall of Temple Beth El in Rochester, New York, there is a wood carving titled "The *Akedah*". Abraham lifts the knife to plunge it into Isaac. But study the carving, as I did, and you will find that there are Abraham and Isaac, but look again and you'll see that they merge into one body, one being. The knife aimed at Isaac will pierce Abraham as well, for they are one. The artist, Hoffman, has not only fashioned a great work of art, but his genius has brought forth a magnificent midrash.

For Abraham, the father, there is no Abraham and Isaac. They are one. It is only through Isaac the son that Abraham the father lives his life and destiny. Without him he is as naught. Isaac's martyrdom is Abraham's as well for Abraham does not exist without him. The father lives only in and through the son. So when Abraham offers up Isaac, he does not offer up another but *himself*!

Tragedy is averted when God's angel reminds and warns Abraham, "Touch not the lad . . . "

He is another against whom you lifted your hand and knife. He is your son tied to you by love and destiny but *he is his own self*!

Parents, good, the best, loving, sacrificing parents who proclaim and exhibit that they have no lives of their own but live only in and through their children. Not for their children, or with their children, but live only in and through their children.

They have no ambitions for themselves, no accomplishment will give them satisfaction, no relationship joy, only that of their children. They deny themselves their own personality and would crush in their children any attempt at individuality. How often I've heard:

"My life is my children," and they mean it in *dead earnest*.

124   What is lacking in their lives they want to see

fulfilled in the lives of children, whether the child wants it or not, needs it or not, can handle it or not. What they have failed to accomplish they demand of their children, and all too often it means failure for one and distress or disaster for the other.

To live with another is lovely. To live for another is noble. To live through another is tragic! Tragic for both.

Abraham, the loving father, the man of faith, of accomplishment, of compassion, had to be reminded that Isaac did not belong to him. Isaac was Isaac.

How often we need to remind ourselves that our Isaacs have their own, their very own, sacred individuality and unique personality. It is so wonderful to behold an Abraham, father, and Isaac, son, sharing, understanding each other, joining in common enterprise, making joint but individual contributions, as Abraham, as Isaac.

We need to live through our own selves, our own resources. Even Abraham had to learn this and learn it the hard way, very hard way. But for this we have the Torah, and the men and women who people it—great, wise, noble men and women, but human, human beings. From their wisdom we can learn. But even more, much more from their humanity, from their shortcomings as much as from their greatness.

"God tested Abraham ten times" says the Midrash. The tenth testing: To offer up his beloved Isaac.

But there was an eleventh testing—the greatest and hardest testing of all.

Raise not your hand against the lad. Release him, let him go.

To deny himself the martyrdom which he craved with all his being, which would give him nobility and distinction, to grant Isaac his own God-given individuality, to do with as he wished, to live his life, and in giving to gain release for self—to begin to live his *own* life—hard, hard thing to do. But this is what life demands!

—Abraham J. Karp 125

WHO WAS TESTED?

The primary sacrifice in the Akedah would appear to be Isaac. After all, it was he who would be asked to surrender his soul. And yet we are told that God tested *Abraham*. Is this the Bible's way of suggesting to us that in the death of a child the parent suffers the greater loss? If this is so, how do we calculate the battlefield losses in war time? Should not we multiply the casualties by two or three to get a more realistic statistic? In counting our Isaacs let us not forget our Abrahams and Sarahs. This more accurate manner of determining our losses should intensify our violent opposition to war.

—Sidney Greenberg

SAND AND STARS

cf. Genesis 22:17

The silver moon shines, and the diamond stars
  twinkle,
Night hovers o'er land and o'er main;
The Book of Creation before me lies open—
I read it again and again.

I read and re-read the old, marvelous stories—
A voice I hear calling to me:
"My people shall be as the stars in the heaven,
As sand on the shore of the sea!"

O heavenly Father, not one of Thy sayings
Has ever proved vain or untrue:
Thy will on the earth, as Thy will in the heaven,
Must come when its season is due.

And half of Thy promise indeed is accomplished:
Thy people became as the sand—
As gloomy and trampled, as humble and wind-tossed,
As scattered on sea and on land.

Yea, half of Thy promise has long been
  accomplished—
Thy people is trodden as sod;
But what of the beauteous, the lofty, the shining,
The heavenly stars, O my God?

—Philip Raskin

GREAT LOYALTY TO LITTLE THINGS

Our generation of American Jews is not being asked to perform any heroic deeds, only little things—and because they are little we are too likely to disregard them.

Being a Jew has too often in our history been fraught with the most fateful consequences and demanded the ultimate in sacrifice and courage. Comfortable and secure as we are in this free and abundant land it is easy to forget the fearful price other generations had to pay for the privilege which is ours for the taking. How many of our forbears died at the stake rather than desert the faith! How many chose exile and the wanderer's staff rather than betray their God. "More impressive" says Maurice Samuel in reviewing the heroic past of our people "was the ability to stand up to the choreography and decor of humiliation which the Middle Ages added to their economic and physical maltreatment of the Jew: the ghetto, the yellow badge, the spitting ceremonials, the insults, the naked foot races, the blood libels, the accusations of poisoning the wells. Hundreds of thousands of little people accepted the verdict of an ever-renewed malevolence without a thought of purchasing security and comfort by defection."

Loyalty to Judaism too frequently was spelled out in acts of martyrdom. Great acts of courage, massive sacrifices were demanded and offered.

But what is demanded of us? Heroism? Martyrdom? Renunciation of home and security? Scarcely! Loyalty to Judaism for us has to be spelled out in humble acts, undramatic tasks, unspectacular little deeds. Beginning the meal with a blessing is a little deed. Abstaining from trefa food is a little deed. Bringing yourself to a service is a little deed. Giving a child a Jewish home, reading a Jewish book, enrolling in a Jewish class—these are quite unspectacular. Lighting the Shabbat candles, reciting the Kiddush, subscribing to a Jewish magazine, buying an Israel Bond, serving on a committee—these are quite undramatic. And yet it is precisely in our faithfulness to these little things that our loyalty to Judaism is reflected, the texture of our lives woven and the very future of Judaism in America determined.

Judaism in America will not be defeated by great acts of betrayal. It will be undermined by small acts of negligence. For want of a nail, the kingdom was lost. Judaism will not be saved by any headline-making, breathtaking deeds of valor. It will be saved by great loyalty to little mitzvot. "Piety," wrote Leo Baeck "especially Jewish piety, respects the little—the little man, the little matter, the little task, the little duty. Through the little, religion meets the greatness that lies behind."

Here then is the heart of the matter. Let us pay large attention to the little things.

—Sidney Greenberg

THE PRECIOUSNESS OF BEING A JEW

I as a Jew do not know what despair is. Despair means utter futility, being utterly lost. I will never be lost. I know where I came from, I know where I am going. I am the son of Abraham. Despite all my imperfections, deficiencies, faults and sins, I remain a part of that Covenant that God made with Abraham; we are going toward the Kingship of God and the Messianic Era. This is the preciousness of being a Jew.

—A.J. Heschel

129

NO SACRIFICE WASTED

In Pirke R. Eliezer, 31 we are told that no particle of the ram which was ultimately used by Abraham went to waste. The ashes were later used to form the foundation of the altar on which atonement was made for Israel. The sinews were used for strings for David's harp. The skin was converted by Elijah into his girdle. One of its horns became the shofar which was sounded at Mount Sinai when the Torah was given and the other horn will be sounded at the end of days.

This picturesque midrash hammers home to us the reassuring conviction that no sacrifice, indeed no portion of a sacrifice is ever wasted. If we achieve without sacrifice in any area it is because of the sacrifice of those who have gone before us. If we sacrifice and see no immediate results we can rest confident in the faith that others will reap the fruits of our exertions. There is a staying power to goodness. The good that men do lives after them. In God's economy nothing good is ever lost. Nothing noble is ever wasted.

—Sidney Greenberg

Let me contrast two scenes for you: two scenes, both
of which are familiar to you—and yet you've probably never thought of them as being in any way
related, nor seen any connection between them.

The first is from the movie, *The Graduate,* which
set so many records and said so many things about
the generation gap just a few years ago. Do you
remember the scene early in the movie, where young
Benjamin has come home from college, and his
parents are giving this big party for him, to which
they've invited all their friends whom he can't stand.
At one point, a friend of his father's comes over, puts
his arm on Benjamin's shoulder and says "I want to
give you one word that will help you become a
success in this world. Just one word." Do you
remember what that word was? "Plastics."

Given what the movie was trying to say, I suspect
that that one word was carefully chosen, to represent
something about his parents' world that Benjamin
rejects. "Plastics" in that context is not just a stock
market tip; it's a way of life. How do you become a
success in this world? By being a plastic person.

You have to be accomodating, willing to change
your shape so that you fit anywhere, prepared to take
on whatever shape and configuration a job demands.
Like plastic, you have to have no form or texture of
your own, except what the outside world gives you,
and be ready to change that too, should circumstances require.

As a plastic person, you have to learn to keep your
cool, be resistant to real emotion. You have to learn
not to get involved, not to get carried away by
feelings. That's what this representative of adult
suburban success passes on to Benjamin as the secret
of life.

The second scene is one we read last week on the
second day of this New Year, the Biblical story of

Abraham leading his son Isaac up the mountain to make a sacrifice of him. The psychoanalyst Theodore Reik, who was a student of Freud, has analyzed that story as the acting out of a "coming of age" ritual of the sort that you find in many cultures. You might facetiously call it "Isaac's Bar Mitzvah." What happens in many societies is that a young boy, on the verge of manhood, is taken out of the community and away from his family, made to undergo a difficult ordeal with hints that his life is at stake. Then when he has shown that he can survive it like a man, the secrets of living as an adult are passed on to him. Reik suggests that this is what the story is about: Isaac is taken away from home, put through this frightening ordeal of being asked to give his life, and when he comes through it, Abraham is assured that Isaac is a worthy heir and successor to his tradition, and tells him what it's all about.

So that you have an astonishing parallel to that scene from *The Graduate*,—an older man who has seen and experienced much of life telling a younger one who has just become an adult, what it means to live and how to succeed in this world. Except that the advice is different. Abraham doesn't tell his son to be a plastic man, accomodating and unemotional. How might he have summarized his advice as to how one lives in this world?

He might have said that real life begins with obligation, with doing something because it has to be done, regardless of whether you feel like doing it or find it convenient. Life is a matter of hearing voices that summon—voices of conscience, voices of community, voices of God in one or another of His manifestations,—and responding to them. At the beginning and at the end of the story, God calls to Abraham and Abraham responds Hineni, Here I am; what is it I have to do? And that's something that only a living person can do. As you have seen, they make plastic dolls that walk and wave and drink, they even make some where you pull a cord and they say something. But they still haven't made a plastic model that can hear and respond, that can react to a challenge with a sense of obligation, of "Here I am, what is it I have to do?"

And yet, that had been the whole story of Abraham's life. And now he was passing on to his son the one great lesson he had absorbed. If you're going to take life seriously, you'll find it very hard, very demanding. Life means having a purpose, a hope, a dream, having a sense that there is something you have to do so that the world will end up somewhere. This is what separated Abraham, who sensed movement and purpose in the world, from his pagan neighbors who believed that life repeats itself endlessly in an unvarying cycle.

I can see Abraham alone with his son on the mountain top, saying to Isaac that people have often mocked us and laughed at us because we wanted something out of life, because we seemed to want more than the world was prepared to give us. We weren't satisfied to have each year a carbon copy of the previous one, each generation a repetition of what had gone on before.

But the hardest part of it wasn't what others thought of us. You know what was the hardest part? That our dream, our goal, meant so much to us, but we could never be sure we'd ever see it. That was the toughest—wanting it and not knowing if it was even possible.

And that's what my belief in God is, my belief that is so different from what the Canaanites and Amalekites around us believe. For them, God is the Great Power in the sky that sends rain and corn and gives them good hunting. For me, God is the assurance that I'm not wrong in basing my life on a hope and a vision. God is the promise that what ought to be in this world, sooner or later will be. And if not my generation, your generation or your children's will live in a better world.

—Harold S. Kushner

133

HAFTARAH

WHY THIS PROPHETIC PORTION WAS CHOSEN

According to the well-known medieval commentator, Rashi, the following passage has been selected for the Haftarah because it graphically depicts the renewal of God's promise to remember Ephraim, His "precious son." The dramatic force of the prophecy is especially great since it comes from Jeremiah, the tragic figure who witnessed the destruction of the Temple in Jerusalem and the exile of his people at the beginning of the sixth century before the Christian era.

There may be yet another reason, for the choice of this prophetic portion. According to one tradition recorded in the Talmud, the future redemption of Israel is to take place on Rosh Hashanah and there are few passages in the entire Bible which describe this deliverance in a more moving and eloquent fashion. Moreover, the message of the everlasting quality of God's love is an especially appropriate form of reassurance on the great *Yom Ha'din,* the Day of Judgment.

At the opening of the chapter, the prophet recalls Israel's golden age, the period immediately following the Exodus from Egypt, when God's gracious care was made manifest to Israel during their perilous wanderings in the desert. The interest is not primarily historical, nor is it a romanticized portrayal of what the Torah describes as a far from idyllic period in the life of our people. It is rather a reminder of God's faithfulness to the covenant—one which recurs throughout the daily liturgy—and an affirmation of God's special relationship to the Jewish people. Furthermore, the prophet asserts, the covenant is grounded in the divine love and, hence, will not be abolished, despite Israel's unworthiness and its many lapses. Suffer it must because of its failure to live up to God's demands of justice and righteousness, but perish it will not because of His boundless compassion and fatherly love!

The prophet stresses two additional factors in the experience of Israel which help keep open its lifeline to God. The first, poignantly depicted in the "weeping of Rachel over her children," is called the doctrine of "the merit of the Fathers." Often appealed to in the liturgy of the High Holy Days, it is in fact a recognition of the importance of the classic Jewish religious heritage, its traditions and practices, its values and heroes, for the continued survival of the Jew and Judaism. The second, also sensitively expressed in the words attributed to Ephraim, is the power of Teshuvah, the basic emphasis of this holiday season.

The Haftarah concludes on an optimistic note, reminding us that the last word is one of hope, of confidence in Israel's future, in man's ability to "return." It thereby reinforces the notion that the Days of Awe are not intended to be occasions for melancholy, pensive brooding over past failures, but rather for a joyous, though solemn, reaffirmation of the possibilities inherent in life, in the world which God has created. It strengthens us in the determination to live by the highest as we know it, even as it gives us the courage to face our own weakness and seek to overcome it.

—David Lieber

135

AN OLD LEGEND,
A LITTLE BOY AND A GREAT MAN

As for me, when I came from Padan, Rachel died.

Genesis 48:7

On this verse Rashi says:

"Even though I am imposing upon you to bring me back to the land of Canaan, I did not accord similar honors to your mother. She died close to Bethlehem and I did not carry her the rest of the way. And so perhaps you might be feeling some resentment because of this, but I want you to know that I did this at the Divine command so that Rachel will be able to help her children in the time to come. When N'vusiradin will drive them into exile they will pass her grave. At that time Rachel will weep and plead for them, as it is said in Jeremiah 31:15, 'A voice is heard in Ramah. Rachel is weeping for her children. She refuses to be comforted because of her children.' Then God will answer her: 'There is reward for your work. Your children shall return to their boundaries.' "

Professor Abraham Sholom Yehuda tells us in one of his books:

Once when I was walking in Madrid in Spain with Max Nordau at the time of the First World War, we were discussing the First Zionist Congress. I told him of the powerful impression made on me by his speech at Basle in one of the Congress sessions. In that talk, given before thousands of people, he discussed the legend on the verse, "Rachel weeps for her children." I asked him how he came by this legend. Had he also learned Humash and Rashi in his youth?

To which Nordau answered: "Some time ago in Paris, when I used to treat patients in my home, a poor Jewish woman came with her eight or nine year old son for treatment. I recognized that the child was quite sharp, but I realized that his French was weak. So I asked him in which school he studied. To which he answered hesitantly and with a little embarrassment that he was studying in a Cheder. And his mother, trying to justify the situation, said that her husband, the father of the boy, is of the older generation who does not want his son to go to the Gentile schools before he finishes his course of studies in Cheder. My feeling towards this old generation at this time was almost one of contempt because he was depriving his son of European culture and it was with a tone of scorn that I asked the child what he was studying in Cheder. The boy became filled with remarkable feeling and he began to tell me in Yiddish Rashi's comment on this verse about Rachel, which he studied in the Cheder on the day before he got sick.

At that moment, Nordau continued, obviously moved himself, my whole body trembled and my heartstrings began to sing a new song. I stood up and embraced this child and kissed him on the forehead, and in my heart I said: "Such a people which preserves such memories for thousands of years and roots them in the hearts of its children, such a people can never die, such a people is assured of eternal life."

This happened, said Nordau, at the time of the Dreyfus affair, when I was beginning to doubt the justice of the nations in their relationship to Israel and I could almost say that this little boy was one of the factors bringing me back to Judaism, to a faith in the eternity of Israel, and to Zionism.

—Sidney Greenberg

REFUSING TO BE COMFORTED

The renowned American novelist Pearl Buck once said that "the primary attitude towards life must be acceptance," and that this acceptance of life is the most significant act of the human mind.

Acceptance is one of the crucial qualities for grown-up living. We have to be able to accept economic losses.

We desperately need the power of acceptance when we, or those we love, sustain a loss of health or become handicapped.

We need the power of acceptance, most urgently, when we sustain the loss of a loved one. How tempting and how human it is to be filled with despair over our possibilities of ever leading a meaningful existence again. Or we can become overwhelmed by self-pity, which has accurately been labeled as "a passport to insanity."

Important as it undeniably is to be able to accept things as they are, there are times when it is no less important to refuse to accept things as they are, when we must reject things as they are, refuse to resign ourselves to the existing situation.

This thought is suggested in this morning's Haftarah. The prophet Jeremiah is addressing himself to the children of Israel, who are in exile in Babylon. He is trying to sustain their hope for eventual restoration to their homeland. He tells them that in Ramah, Rachel's burial place, a voice is heard weeping and lamenting. It is the voice of mother Rachel crying over the bitter destiny of her exiled children. And the prophet adds the striking phrase: *"Meyanah l'hin-ahem*—She refuses to be comforted." She refuses to resign herself to the thought of permanent exile. She refuses to accept the fact of her children's eternal homelessness.

You can offer any explanation you wish for the miracle of reborn Israel. For myself, I am quite willing to sum it up in these two Hebrew words: *"Meyanah l'hinahem."* Our people refused to be comforted over exile. Other peoples before them and after them were driven out of their homeland. They shrugged their shoulders in an attitude of despair and proceeded to accept their new circumstances. The Jew alone refused to accept his new situation as permanent. Seventy-nine consecutive generations refused to be comforted. They fasted and wept on *Tisha b'Av,* and in a hundred other ways reminded themselves regularly of their resolve to return. That resolve became a fact in our time because they refused to accept things as they were.

This, of course, is true of every noteworthy human achievement. Trace back any worthwhile discovery or invention far enough, whether in medicine or technology or in any field of human endeavor, and you will find its origin in the heart of a man who was disturbed and refused to be comforted, refused to accept things as they were.

George Bernard Shaw conveyed this thought with characteristic wit: "The reasonable man," he said, "adapts himself to the world. The unreasonable one persists in trying to adapt the world to himself. Therefore, all progress depends on the unreasonable man."

In this sense, it is of vital importance that we become unreasonable. I submit that there are three decisive areas where we are too easily resigned, too prone to accept things as they are. In each of these, Judaism commands that we refuse to be comforted. These three areas are reflected in three brief prayers at the beginning of our Rosh Hashanah Amidah, each of which is introduced by the word *uvhen.*

The first *uvhen* expresses the hope that all nations might form a single union—that there might indeed be a genuine United Nations.

Let us refuse to be reconciled to a tension-torn world until we have expended every available effort to fulfill the first *uvḥen*—"Let all nations form a single community to do Thy will with a perfect heart."

The second *uvḥen* asks: "*Tayn kavod l'amecha*— Grant honor to Thy people." It expresses our prayer for the restoration of dignity to the Jew, a sense of self-esteem and self-respect.

The last *uvḥen* embodies the hope that we may soon see the day "when wickedness shall vanish like smoke." If we want to see wickedness disappear in the world, I suppose that we ought to begin with the wickedness within ourselves.

It is noteworthy that our opening text from Jeremiah, which pictures mother Rachel weeping disconsolately and refusing to accept comfort, goes on to tell us that Rachel does receive a magnificent promise from God: "Refrain thy voice from weeping and thine eyes from tears, for thy work shall be rewarded. . . Thy sons shall return to their own borders. There is hope for thy future." By refusing to accept superficial comfort, by refusing to reconcile herself to a situation which cries out for redress and which can in fact be redeemed, Rachel is promised the higher comfort—the ultimate end to the exile and a glorious homecoming for her children.

As long as we refuse to accept as final a divided humanity, a dejudaized Jewish community and our own unredeemed lives and we translate that dissatis- faction into an incessant struggle against these evils, then can we, too, hope to hear the reassuring promise of God: "There is hope for thy future."

Our theme can be summed up in the humble words of the man who prayed: "Dear God, grant us the serenity to accept the things we cannot change, the courage to change the things we can change, and the wisdom to know one from the other."

140

—Sidney Greenberg

ONE OF THEM IS MISSING

Mayanah lihinahem al baneha kee aynenu cannot mean "she refuses to be comforted for her children *for they are not*" as the English Bible renders it. Aynenu cannot mean "they are not." "They are not" would be aynam. Aynenu is the singular form, and means "*he* is not". The only acceptable translation which accords with syntax is therefore "She refuses to be comforted for her children, *for one of them is missing.*" It gives an entirely new meaning to the verse.

Imagine a mother who has six children who have all left her. Five of them ultimately return home while the sixth is still estranged and away. Is there a Jewish mother who will not mourn and yearn and weep bitter tears for that one child who is still away from the fold? All the consolation and joy which she finds in the five will not staunch her tears for the sixth, until it is enfolded again in her arms. That, I am convinced, is the meaning of this verse.

The prophet sees the *Shivat Zion* fulfilled; all the verses which precede this one have become a fact, but in the midst of the general jubilation and joy, Mother Rachel still weeps. She wants all her children back, all without exception, and aynenu, *there is one that is missing*, and she stands in desperate need of the blessed assurance that yet " *all Your children* will return to their border" and then only will she find consolation and joy.

—Louis Rabinowitz

A LIBERATING DOCTRINE

Jeremiah 31:17

The High Holy Days are serious occasions for they direct our thoughts to important and even crucial questions and seek to arouse us to make profound and transforming decisions. The truth is that this season is saturated with the deep optimism which characterizes the Jewish outlook upon life.

Our faith rejects on the one hand the fatalism by which the ancient Greeks saw life governed, and on the other the belief that man is ineradicably stained by evil from which he cannot free himself by the exercise of his own will and determination.

Judaism is realistic enough to recognize that man is inevitably bound by restrictions within and without. He is mortal and he may not in this life step beyond the circle which this fact draws around him. He lives in a world which hedges him about with definite limitations. His constitution imposes upon him boundaries beyond which he cannot venture.

Yet Judaism emphasizes that within the circumference of restrictions man enjoys a measure of freedom which is decisive in establishing the quality of his life. Goodness and nobility, character and high values are within man's reach and by his resolve he may attain them. No circumstances outside of him and no drives within him automatically dictate the level in which his life as a human being shall be led. Neither the world nor his own nature can deprive him of his sovereign power to determine the moral and human quality of his career on earth. When man says "the forces of life are too much for me," he abdicates the basic freedom which is his as an individual.

This is as liberating and cheering a doctrine as any religion may contribute to the thought and happiness of its adherents. We are free, we matter and in the most significant sense our life is in our own hands. This is the message of this season. Though none of us is without sin, yet none of us need surrender to hopelessness. We are not here acting out a script that has been written for us. We are co-authors of the story of our life and should resolutely bear our responsibility for it. It is a responsibility which gives us the precious opportunity to revise, edit, renew, and construct the drama in which we have the principal part.

Let us be worthy of such an opportunity.

—Morris Adler

A NEW BEGINNING CAN ALWAYS BE MADE

Jeremiah 31:17

The buoyant optimism of Judaism in teaching that a new beginning can always be made feels strange in our day and age. The fashionable philosophies of our time speak of anxiety and frustration, of failure and despair, of man's "creaturely" helplessness and "existential" tragedy, of the knell of doom in the distance, sounding dark and implacable. But we must remember that the message of Judaism always sounds strange to human ears. Even in the ages of faith, when men walked about with long pious faces, mortifying their flesh in penitence and contorting their minds to fit rigid dogmas, the healthy optimism of our faith sounded strange and unbelievable. For Judaism is healthy minded and open-eyed. It does not close its eyes to evil in nature or to sin in human nature, but it asserts with tireless persistence that God is "King" over nature and that man is capable of triumphing over the evil in his makeup. "It is at the door that sin lurks, lusting for you, but you may rule over it." (Gen. 4:7)

—Jacob B. Agus

144

THE HOPE AND THE FULFILLMENT

cf. Jeremiah 31:17

We approach the New Year in our calendar with mixed emotions of hope and trepidation. There is always something exciting about the unknown, and there is an unquenchable optimism in human hearts which creates the hope that things to come will be different and better. "Wait till next year" is a slogan that we frequently use to bolster our drooping spirits and to cover our recurring failures. How the New Year will be different or better we are not sure—but somehow we make ourselves believe that new conditions, new circumstances will arise that will improve our fortunes.

At the same time, we cannot escape the melancholy thought that unless we take things in our hands, effect certain changes in the pattern of our lives, the New Year is not going to be any different than the old year and instead of getting better, matters may well get worse. We have been taught, "one must not rely on miracles", and if we are to improve our lot in life, if we are to achieve anything of significance for ourselves—we must not yield to blind faith and optimism but must fashion our fate by our own initiative and action.

Rosh Hashanah summons us to such action, to self-renewal and to regeneration. It assures us that the New Year can be better for us, that our circumstances can change and the pattern of our lives can improve. We are not doomed to stay the way we are; we are not trapped by fate or destiny to be permanently cast in the mold in which we find ourselves. There is hope, great hope for us in the unknown future that the New Year unfolds before us. But it is a hope conditioned on the role that we are prepared to play in the drama

145

of life. We cannot be passive spectators expecting things to happen to us or be done for us. We are cast in major roles and we must act them out in full confidence that what we say and do will determine the success of our efforts.

May the New Year find us all prepared to enrich the content of our lives, ready to meet all the challenges ahead, and hopeful that, with God's help, our tasks and duties will be blessed with rich fulfillment and with achievements.

—Max J. Routtenberg

Despite the assurance of Shakespeare I have never been successful in finding sermons in stones, although I have given sermons which have evoked stony responses. Nor have I found trees having tongues nor discovered books in the running brooks. However, in the Shakespearian spirit, I recently found a sermon in running that brooks no dispute.

As a practitioner of the sport of sports—watching, I have noticed athletic records falling one by one in the Olympic try-outs. The 4-minute mile, which was once a barrier to the greatest milers, has been breached so frequently that there are by now scores of runners who have managed it. The shot-put record has, in thirty-five years, gone from 52 feet to over 71 feet. The 15-foot, 16-foot and 17-foot barriers in pole-vaulting have been successively and successfully overcome by many athletes.

What is true in track is true in a hundred different fields. In science and technology barriers are being daily overcome. There must be a sermon and a moral in these circumstances.

Clearly, man is progressively capable of making the impossible possible. No one can even begin to set a limit to human capabilities. But what is more significant is that once a barrier is breached by one man, scores, hundreds and even thousands suddenly become equally capable. Apparently, all we need is one breakthrough for the impossible not only to become possible, but routine.

The one great exception to this rule is in the area of human relations. The barriers which stand in the way of decency, cooperation, justice and love seem to yield very slowly to man's assault. Perhaps we do not try hard enough; perhaps the psychological barriers

147

are greater. We have, of course, made major break-throughs over the course of the centuries, but not as decisively and as effectively as we have in so many other fields.

Both the failure and the possibility are problems to meditate upon in the High Holiday season. If Judaism has one central message, it is that breakthroughs in the realm of the spirit are always possible. It is that possibility which we assert and celebrate on Rosh Hashanah and Yom Kippur.

Beyond the message lies a faith. Once such break-throughs are achieved by a substantial group of people, the possibilities that will open up before mankind are limitless. Perhaps the whole Messianic idea is no more than the notion that some day man will breach the four minute barrier on spiritual race tracks.

The analogy I have been drawing between races over cinder paths and races over impalpable tracks has a special merit this year when the Olympics are being held in Mexico City at a very high altitude. Men's athletic capabilities are going to be tested more than they ever have been before. In the realm of human values and behavior also, this is an Olympic year. We are running a race in the midst of the most desperate circumstances we have encountered in long centuries and the need is for a record-breaking response, greater than has ever been demanded of us in the past. The great question is—can we run successfully at high altitudes?

—Mordecai Waxman

THE FINAL FORM OF LOVE

cf. Jeremiah 31:17

Nothing that is worth doing can be achieved in our lifetime; therefore we must be saved by hope.

Nothing which is true or beautiful or good makes complete sense in any immediate context of history; therefore we must be saved by faith.

Nothing we do, however virtuous, can be accomplished alone; therefore we are saved by love.

No virtuous act is quite as virtuous from the standpoint of our friend or foe as it is from our standpoint. Therefore we must be saved by the final form of love which is forgiveness.

—Reinhold Niebuhr

OUR HOPES KEEP US ALIVE

cf. Jeremiah 31:17

How careful we must be to resist the counsels of despair and cynicism and discouragement which may rob us of our most precious hopes. When we surrender our hopes, we surrender the possibilities of improving life, of changing circumstances, of planning ahead constructively and creatively. Life itself becomes a burden if there are no wings of hope to sustain it.

Picture the world community without hope. If we accept wars as final and inevitable, hatreds between nations built into the very fabric of human society, oppression and aggression a basic and ineradicable part of the inheritance that man brought with him from the jungle; if we consider the prophet's vision of a world community rooted in justice, living by righteousness and blessed with peace—if all that is simply the delusion of an incurable idealist without any possibility of being translated into reality, then, of course, we should withdraw from the United Nations, we should stop sending aid and relief to underdeveloped nations, we should exclaim, "Stop the world, we want to get off!"

Picture the Jewish community without hope. If we accept the verdict emanating from some quarters that there is no future for Judaism in America, that it will undergo a slow, painless but inevitable dissolution, that Jewish ignorance and assimilation and intermarriage will grow ever larger until they prove fatal—if we accept all this as the last word, then of course all our Synagogues and our Hebrew Schools and our Camps Ramah and our Jewish homes are all empty monuments of futility, and the better part of wisdom would be to give up, to throw in the *tallit* and to announce to the world that the 3500 year old drama has come to an end.

150   Picture us as human beings without hope. A.J.

Cronin has written, "Hell is the place where one has ceased to hope." Life without hope is an unending nightmare. If we could not hope for a second chance when life inflicts a severe defeat on us, if we could not hope for strength when we have been betrayed, if we could not hope for wisdom when we are confused, if we could not hope for healing when we have been bruised, if we could not hope for consolation when we have been bereaved, if we could not hope for eternity when the imminence of winter drives home the inescapable fact of our mortality, if in all these trials hope should not well up within our breasts—the burden of life would become insufferable. Let us beware of those who would rob us of our hopes.

To be a Jew means to be what Yehuda Halevi once called "a prisoner of hope." We have been nourished by it and kept alive by it. How else could we have survived in the face of all the evil designs that were spun against us! We are a people whose anthem is "Hatikvah," which means "The Hope." We are a people who repeat thrice daily—"*Al kayn nekaveh l'cha*—We, therefore, *hope* in Thee, O Lord, our God." We are a people who greet death with the Kaddish, in which we look forward to the establishment of God's kingdom of peace throughout the world.

And because we are "prisoners of hope" we do believe in the possibility of a world community living in brotherhood and in peace; we do believe in a Jewish community distinguished by a knowledge of its heritage, loyalty to its traditions and commitment to its ideals. And because we are "prisoners of hope" we permit neither failure, nor perplexity, nor sorrow, nor death to defeat us.

"Hope," some one has said with great justice, "is the promissory note of life on which the principal never matures but which pays compound interest to those who render their best services each day." Let us treasure carefully our hopes. They keep us alive.

—Sidney Greenberg   *151*

YESH TIKVAH: THE OPTIMISM OF JUDAISM

cf. Jeremiah 31:17

Judaism did not dwell, in the exclusive way of Christianity, on bliss in the afterworld, nor did it consider that the Messianic manifestation at the end of days would be a "day of wrath and destruction." Steadfastness would ultimately receive its reward—*in this world*; a state of perfection would ultimately be attained—*in this world*. Thus there was in the Jewish outlook an inherent optimism. It believed in the perfectibility of humanity. It considered that to despair of redemption was one of the sins that would not be forgiven at Judgment Day. It thought of the Golden Age as being in the future, not in the past. The worse external conditions grew, the more profound and deep-rooted was the certainty of deliverance—and if we examine Jewish history in detail, we see that those few Jewish people who succumbed to the pressure of the environment did so not because they suffered more than the others, but because they gave up the optimistic conviction of ultimate deliverance. It was a conviction that in later times made it natural for Jews to take a prominent part in movements for the abolition of war and the establishment of universal peace, indeed, in many movements aimed at improving the lot of mankind. This optimistic outlook is of the greatest significance too for the present age, when scientific developments have given a grim actuality to Christian conceptions of the Last Day and the destruction of the world. As against this, Judaism teaches that to despair of the future is one of the gravest of all sins, because the perfect age, for which every man must work, still lies before us.

—Cecil Roth

DESPITE EVIDENCE TO THE CONTRARY

cf. Jeremiah 31:17

In the ruins of the Warsaw Ghetto a most remarkable document was discovered. It is a composite scientific report of some 22 Jewish doctors who together with their wives and children were systematically and slowly starved to death by the Nazis. When these physicians realized the fate that awaited them they determined to make a study of the effects of starvation on the human mind and body. With incredible objectivity they recorded the pathological changes, the emotional reactions, the speed of reflexes in their starving wives and children, and in themselves. As each doctor in turn met his own inescapable fate the manuscript was passed along to the next one. The last surviving physician buried the manuscript in the flaming ruins of the crumbling ghetto in the hope that some day this study would be unearthed and the scientific findings which it contained might contribute to the store of human knowledge. None of the physicians survived but what they did collectively was an enduring testament to their belief, in the face of the most crushing evidence to the contrary, that life has a meaning and a purpose which even the bestiality of the Nazis could not destroy.

—Sidney Greenberg

I JUST KNOW

cf. Jeremiah 31:17

We must never despair of any man, at any time. The doors of *teshuvah* (repentance) are always open. No matter how far one has wandered from Torah, no matter how thoroughly one seems to have alienated himself from that divine investment in his own being, we must always have confidence in the sudden, miraculous rekindling of that dark ember of Jewishness within him. *Ki lo yidach mimenu nidach*—we must never concede the loss of any Jew to Judaism.

Right after the recent Six Day War in Israel, the evening paper *Yediot Acharonot* carried the following report to it by the vigorously anti-religious author, Aharon Amir, identified with the "Canaanites." He tells of a conversation between his young daughter and himself:

"God," she emphatically and with certainty declared, "God is looking after us."

"God!?"

"Yes."

I was utterly astonished. I thought for a moment and then posed a further question:

"Who told you? Nadav?"

Nadav is my older son. He is already nine and in grade three.

"Yes," answered the child in simple faith.

Afterwards I cross-examined my son and told him all about my conversation with his baby sister and the final triumphant retort that she had attributed to his wisdom.

"You told her that God is looking after us?"

"Yes," he answered simply.

"And who told you? The teacher?"

"No. No one."

154   "Then who told you?"

"No one. Just myself."

"How do you know?"

"I know. I *just know*."

In those three words from the mouth of a nine-year-old, "I just know," we have the finest proof of what R. Shneour Zalman of Ladi, founder of the Chabad movement within Hasidism, has called *ahavah tiv'it u-mesuteret*, "the natural and concealed love (of God)," the indomitable and irrepressible religious urge, the unconquerable sense of Jewishness, that bespeaks man's enormous spiritual potential, which derives from his essential sanctity, his value, his worth.

Wherefrom my obstinate optimism that all Jews will eventually return to Torah—as Maimonides put it (in his *Hil. Teshuvah* 4:2), *she'bi'zeman she'yaasu teshuvah*, "when" the community will return to Torah, not only "if?" I JUST KNOW.

Wherefrom my unwillingness to concede that any young Jew or Jewess, no matter what his or her sudden sophistication at being exposed to the wide, wide academic world in the universities, and his or her first brush with pungent and polysyllabic *apikorsut*—my unwillingness to acknowledge that such a person is irretrievably lost? My faith that with greater wisdom and more experience there will be this *teshuvah*, this return? I JUST KNOW.

Why this persistence of the Halakhah that *yisrael af-al-pi she'chata yisrael hu*, that no matter how much a Jew has sinned he remains a Jew—a doctrine often heatedly rejected by Jews who refuse to remain identified as Jews and who consider this principle racist and undemocratic? It is because we and the whole Jewish tradition "just know" that man is both biologically and spiritually worthy, and that as the handiwork of the Creator is always redeemable.

—Norman Lamm

YOUR CHILDREN SHALL RETURN

In the light of recent history, it is probable that the contemporary worshipper will be impressed most by the verses, " . . . and they shall come back from the land of the enemy . . . thy children shall return to their own border." These prophetic words have been fulfilled in epic proportions before our eyes. The Zionist movement, on the one hand, and the persecution of tyrants, on the other, combined to restore to their ancestral borders hundreds of thousands of Jews who had been dispersed in "the land(s) of the enemy." Moreover, many Jewish artists, intellectuals and men of affairs have reacted to their people's epic martyrdom and rebirth by returning to the spiritual fold of Israel, if not to its soil.

Many gifted but alienated sons of Israel won great renown among the nations in their chosen fields, only to suffer disillusionment and to return to serve their own folk and faith. Theodor Herzl, urbane journalist, Moses Hess, the Marxist, and Max Nordau, critic of Europe's decadent civilization, become leaders of the new Zionist movement. Franz Rosenzweig turned his philosophic gifts from Hegel to Torah and helped a bewildered generation of German Jews to reaccept their Jewish heritage; his influence is latterly being felt in American Jewish circles once far removed from the ancestral faith.

Walter Rathenau, the brilliant statesman of Weimar Germany, who had rebelled against Judaism in his youth, toward middle age took up the study of Hebrew and began to return to the faith of his fathers, guided by the master-theologian, Martin Buber. Shortly before his murder by Nazi thugs, Rathenau wrote: "After an estrangement of twenty years, I am back with my people. I have come to be one of them again, to participate in the celebration of the holidays, to share the memories and hopes of a nation, to take part in the spiritual and intellectual warfare going on within the house of Israel, on the one hand, and between our own people and the surrounding civilized world on the other."

Of Max Nordau's return to Jewish loyalties, his gifted daughter has written:

I shall never forget the day, so strange to me, when I saw my father, the author of "Conventional Lies," the atheist, carrying the Scrolls of the Law, his shoulders wrapped in the *tallith*. The small Jewish community in the Spanish capital had obtained—not without difficulty—the right to open a synagogue in a back yard. They asked father to inaugurate it and he consented as a token of solidarity, as a step toward unity among the Jews. The long-forgotten words of prayer came back to his lips and in his innermost soul there must have been a deep gratitude for that unique moment of communion.

—Herman Kieval

YOUR CHILDREN SHALL RETURN

In Rachel's tomb in Bethlehem there is a mosaic on one of the walls which consists of the verses from Jeremiah which tell of Rachel's weeping and God's consolation that her children will return to their own border. The mosaic is signed, "This was made by one of her children who returned."

—Sidney Greenberg

157

THERE IS HOPE FOR YOUR FUTURE

The Haftarah for the second day of Rosh Hashanah carries heavy accents of promise and hope. The buoyant mood of the prophet can be a springboard for examining the role of faith and hope in our lives.

We master fear through faith—faith in the worthwhileness of life and the trustworthiness of God; faith in the meaning of our pain and our striving, and confidence that God will not cast us aside but will use each one of us as a piece of priceless mosaic in the design of His universe.

—Joshua Loth Liebman

When all else is lost, the future still remains.

—C. N. Bovee

No ray of sunlight is ever lost, but the green which it wakes into existence needs time to sprout, and it is not always granted to the sower to live to see the harvest. All work that is worth anything is done in faith.

—Albert Schweitzer

Fear builds prison walls around a man and bars him in with dreads, anxieties and timid doubts. Faith is the great liberator from prison walls. Fear paralyzes, faith empowers; fear disheartens, faith encourages, fear sickens, faith heals; fear puts hopelessness at the heart of life, while faith sees beyond the horizon and rejoices in its God.

—Lewis L. Dunnington

Every tomorrow has two handles. We can take hold of it by the handle of anxiety or the handle of faith.

—Author Unknown

Faith, you can do very little with it, but you can do nothing without it.

—Samuel Butler

Faith is knowing there is an ocean because you have seen a brook.

—William A. Ward

On the wall of a cellar in Cologne, where a number of escaped prisoners hid out for the duration, there was found this inscription: "I believe in the sun, even when it is not shining. I believe in love, even when feeling it not. I believe in God, even when He is silent."

—Louis Binstock

When God wants to punish a man, He deprives him of faith.

—The Baal Shem Tov

You may be deceived if you trust too much, but you will live in torment if you do not trust enough.

—Frank Crane

History is on the side of faith—not fear.

—Author Unknown

159

Man lives by affirmation even more than he does by bread.

—Victor Hugo

The dynamite of doubt is useful in wrecking old structures; but to build new buildings, we must have the dynamics of faith.

—Joseph L. Baron

FIRST AND SECOND DAY OF ROSH HASHANAH

MAFTIR READING, Numbers 29:1-6

Editor's Note

The Maftir reading for both days of Rosh Hashanah describes the sacrifices which were offered in the Temple in ancient times. Hence the theme of *"sacrifice"* can be linked to this Torah portion.

In addition, the reference in the opening verse to *Yom T'ruah* justifies treatment of the Shofar theme.

The reading from the second scroll consists of the Torah passage Numbers 29:1-6. Nowhere in the Talmud is a reading from a second scroll prescribed for Rosh Hashanah. The first mention of this practice is in the *Seder of R. Amram* (9th century C.E.). The talmudist, Mordecai ben Hillel (13th century C.E.), suggests that a sanction for this reading from the second scroll might be discerned in this talmudic statement: "After the destruction of the Temple, the act of reading the Torah portion describing the sacrifices prescribed for the paticular day was accounted to the people as if the sacrifices had actually been offered . . . " (Taan. 27b).

Where only one scroll is available, the second portion is read from the same scroll. But it is a rule that one must avoid a tedious unrolling of a scroll from one portion to another portion "out of respect for the congregation" (Yoma 70a). Rashi (*ibid.*) explains the passage to mean that the congregation would have to wait in silence while the scroll is being rolled to the proper passage. For this reason a second scroll is taken out. That the reading of the portion dealing with the sacrifices of the day is not a prescribed one can be seen from the fact that it is only a *Maftir* portion and is not reckoned among the number of *aliyot* prescribed for the Torah reading either on Rosh Hashanah, Yom Kippur, or the Festivals.*

In the instructions for the sacrifices offered on all other holidays and festivals, the term used is *vehikravtem olah* "and you shall offer a burnt offering."

*Saul Lieberman, *Tosefta Ki-Fshutah, Moed* (New York: The Jewish Theological Seminary of America, 1962), p. 1171.

But in prescribing the burnt offering for Rosh Hashanah, the Torah uses the term *veasitem olah* "and you shall make a burnt offering." This variation inspires the comment that on Rosh Hashanah it is man's opportunity to become spiritually renewed: "On this day I shall transform you into new persons" (TP R. H. 59c).

The Hebrew language has no exact equivalent for the term New Year. Rosh Hashanah means literally, the beginning of the year. In a sense, the year is not new. Not the year, but each individual must become as new. Life can be a progress and unfolding of moral and intellectual growth, or it can be purposeless. The choice is man's, but it is for God to judge that choice—to approve it, or to rebuke it. Man can become a "new personality" if he remembers the psalmist's prayer, "So teach us to number our days that we may get us a heart of wisdom" (Ps. 90:12), and if he considers each day a fresh occasion on which to mature his judgment and to refine his sensibilities.

—Max Arzt

ON THE IDEA OF SACRIFICES

There are many who see no point in continuing readings such as this in view of the fact that the sacrificial system has been obsolete in Judaism for 1900 years. There is an element of embarrassment for the primitive tone of such verses. (Even Maimonides interpreted the cult of animal sacrifice as a concession by Moses to the tastes of his own period.) Instructive, then, is the wise observation of Isaac Arama, eminent Jewish thinker of medieval Spain and author of the influential Torah commentary, *Akaydat Yitzhak*: "If we have a true understanding of the Jewish religion, then not one iota of religious practice has ever been abandoned. The sacrifices have ceased but the *idea* of sacrifices has never ceased."

From Talmudic times down to the last century, the majority of Jewish children received their first impressions of Jewish literature through the opening chapters of the book of Leviticus that deal exclusively with the sacrificial system. This practice has been ridiculed by modern pedagogues, a situation which elicited this delightful rebuttal from Solomon Schechter:

> The Jew of ancient times was not given to analysis. Seizing upon its bold features, he saw in the Book of Leviticus only the good message of God's reconciliation with man, by means of sacrifice and of purity in soul and body. Perceiving, on the other hand, in every babe the budding minister "without taint of sin and falsehood," the Rabbi could certainly render no higher homage to childhood than when he said, "Let the pure come and busy themselves with purity." Every school thus assumed in his eyes the aspect of a holy Temple, in which the child by his reading performed the service of an officiating priest.

Another beautiful interpretation of the spiritual significance of the sacrificial worship is given by the Midrash. It reminds us that the animals offered up are tame, from among the persecuted and not the persecutors, just as Israel is among the persecuted rather than the persecuting peoples. Scripture states, "God seeks that which is pursued" (Ecclesiastes 3:15). The Midrash comments: "God always avenges the innocent blood of the pursued from the pursuers . . . . therefore offer not unto Me the persecutors but the persecuted.

—Herman Kieval

On both days of Rosh Hashanah, we read a passage from the second scroll, describing the sacrifices that were offered up on the Holy Days. This practice seems to have been adopted during the early middle ages, on the grounds that "the act of reading the Torah portion describing the sacrifices . . . was accounted to the people as if the sacrifices had actually been offered. . . "

The rites, themselves, were part of the cult rooted in antiquity in which our ancestors sought to draw near to God by bringing Him their most precious possessions. Accompanied by orchestras of Levites and choruses of Temple singers, the priests offered up the animals in the presence of throngs of worshippers. The deep impression these services made can readily be seen from many of the psalms which were composed by the faithful who participated in them.

With the destruction of the Second Temple, a new mode of worship came into being—prayer. While we ourselves no longer respond to the ancient rites, we are impressed by the spirit of piety they evoked among our ancestors and seek to keep it alive in our midst. Moreover, we recognize that prayer itself must not merely be a matter of the lips, but an expression of the peak moments of a life lived in the presence of God, a life prepared to make sacrifices in order to draw closer to Him, the Creator of all blessings and the source of all good.

—David Lieber

THE RATIONALIZATION OF THE SACRIFICIAL CULT

As long as the Temple existed, the sacrificial rites were regularly performed and the cult retained its unchallenged position. No one questioned that it was God's will that He be worshipped by means of this ceremonial. However, when the Temple was destroyed and the sacrificial cult became only a historic memory, the rabbis sensed the incongruity of divine worship by means of slaughtering animals, sprinkling blood on the altar, and similar priestly rituals. Yet they accepted the Temple cult as a divine service. How could they do otherwise-is it not commanded in the Torah? The rabbis therefore reexamined the Temple ritual from their own vantage point. They "searched" in the text and found an answer to their perplexing problem. They discovered in the sacrificial rites unsuspected religious and ethical teachings.

Why, ask the rabbis, is it commanded in the Torah that the meal-offering should be of fine flour mingled with oil? To teach us that our daily life (which is compared to flour) should be mingled with the ethical teachings of the Torah (which is compared to oil).* And why are the crop and feathers removed from a bird offering (Lev. 1:16), while an animal is offered up whole (Lev. 1:13)? Because the bird flies and eats food which is not its master's while the domesticated animal is reared on the master's crib. This is to teach us that the worshipper must be clean from the stains of violence and robbery.**

Philo, the Alexandrian Jewish philosopher who lived at the turn of the first century of the Common

---

*J. Israel Stam and Judah J. Slotki, transl. *"Midrash Rabbah on Leviticus"* (London, 1939) p. 44.

**Ibid., pp. 38-39.

Era, similarly interpreted the sacrificial rites. The animals chosen for sacrifices, said Philo, are the meek of the animal kingdom. This is to teach us that God loves the humble and rejects the proud and the aggressive. The provision that the victim must be without blemish is to teach us that he who worships God must strive for perfection and his conduct must be irreproachable.

Obviously not every detail of the ritual could be infused with symbolic meaning of a spiritual nature. But this did not disturb the rabbis. The absence of significant meaning was in itself a spiritual lesson; it taught the duty to obey God's commandments even when one could not grasp their significance. Obedience of God's Torah is in itself a principle of transcendent value.

—Abraham E. Millgram

NO RELIGION IS WORTH ITS SALT UNLESS . . .

No religion is worth its salt which does not make great demands upon its adherents. The greatest enthusiasm was always engendered by faiths which called for the greatest sacrifices on the part of their devotees who received in return great compensation and satisfaction which their souls desired. According to our tradition, increased merit and worth were bestowed upon Israel through the very abundance of the commandments which were given to it. Too many of our people want an easy-going religion, one which does not interfere with their leisure, their sleep, or their television, which calls for no study and no observance, which does not challenge or disturb them, a religion without any spiritual travail, without any stab of thought or conscience, without any sacrifices, the religion of a self-pampering people. No religion has ever survived in that kind of an emotional and intellectual vacuum, Judaism least of all.

—Abba Hillel Silver

The Maggid of Dubno, in keeping with the injuction in *Mishnah Abot* 2.13, "Do not let your prayers become perfunctory," frequently exhorted his hearers to perform their devotions on the High Holy Days with understanding and reverence, and not by rote. He reminded them that fulfilling the rituals was a means to a higher end, namely, to achieve an inner purification.

To dramatize the nobler objective, he related this graphic parable:

A naive villager, born and reared in an obscure rural environment, came to a big city for the first time and obtained lodging at an inn. Awakened in the middle of the night by the loud beating of drums, he inquired drowsily, "What's this all about?" Informed that a fire had broken óut and that the drum beating was the city's fire alarm, he turned over and went back to sleep.

On his return home he reported to the village authorities: "They have a wonderful system in the big city; when a fire breaks out the people beat their drums and before long the fire burns out." All excited, they ordered a supply of drums and distributed them to the population. When a fire broke out later, there was a deafening explosion of beating of drums, and while the people waited expectantly for the flames to subside, a number of their homes burned to the ground.

A sophisticated visitor passing through that village, when told the reason for the ear-splitting din, derided the simplistic natives: "Idiots! Do you think a fire can be put out by beating drums? They only sound an alarm for the people to wake up and take measures to extinguish the fire."

171

This parable, said the Maggid of Dubno, applies to those of us who believe that beating the breast during the *Al Het* (confessional), raising our voices during worship, and blowing the *shofar* will put out the fires of sin and evil that burn in us. They are only an alarm, a warning to wake up and resort to *heshbon ha-nefesh* (soul-searching), so that we may merit the favor of God. The Maggid probably had in mind Maimonides' interpretation of the *shofar* sounds as urging: "Awake all ye who sleep, rouse yourselves all ye who slumber and search your deeds and repent; remember your Creator."

—Translated by Alexander A. Steinbach

In the Torah, the first mention of the *shofar* is in the
account of the revelation at Sinai: "And it came to
pass, on the third day, when it was morning, that
there were thunders and lightnings and a thick cloud
upon the mount, and the voice of a horn (*shofar*)
exceeding loud; and all the people that were in the
camp trembled" (Exod. 19:16). Since this is the first
of the *Shofarot* verses, the prelude to the *Shofarot*
consists of a stirring retelling of that which transpired
at Sinai. The prelude focuses our attention on the
extraordinary nature of that revelation. God revealed
Himself not to the chosen few, but to an entire
people—"to teach Thy people *Torah* and *Mitzvot*."
Yehezkel Kaufmann, in his monumental study of the
religion of the Bible, points to the stunning original-
ity of the idea that an entire people was the
recipient and vehicle of God's revelation. The concept
implies that the moral law is to be regarded not as the
doctrine of sages or the dictate of earthly rulers, but
as the will of God made known to an entire people
consecrated to be "a kingdom of priests, and a holy
nation" (Exod. 19:6). Israel is a people not thrown
together by accidental circumstances, but drawn
together by an indissoluble covenant with God—a
covenant that might be defied, but not denied;
broken, but not annulled. Throughout history this
people was haunted by the memory of its corporate
commitment, and inwardly plagued by its all too
frequent backsliding from provisions of the covenant.

One would expect such a fixation on one event in
the past to produce a static and monolithic conception of the character and content of the revelation.
But the very notion that the whole people was the
vehicle of divine revelation saved Judaism from an
arid, literal biblicism. It gave rise to the belief that the
"oral law" is the authentic and living interpretation
of the "written law," so that Revelation came to be

173

regarded as a continuing process. The Rabbis seem to have grasped intuitively an idea akin to the modern concept of historical evolution, when they asserted that at Sinai both the oral and the written laws were revealed. Rabbi Haggai even went so far as to say that the oral teachings took precedence over those that were written (TP Peah 17a), and that all the teachings of future scholars were revealed to Moses on Mt. Sinai (ibid.). Judaism's hospitality to the idea that Revelation is a cumulative process is reflected in this interesting passage:

"They (the sayings of the wise) are given from one shepherd" (Eccl. 12:14). The Holy One, blessed is He, said: "If a person of modest scholarly attainments tells you something and you derive spiritual delight from his insight, do not regard it as something you heard from an inferior scholar. Moreover, you must even regard it as having been told you by a great sage. And even more than that! You must regard it as having been heard from the mouth of a prophet, and even beyond that, you must regard it as if you had heard it from Moses himself . . . . and even much more than that! You must regard it as if you have heard it from God himself" (TP Sanh. 28a).

An even bolder extension of the idea of Revelation is implied in the statement that where scholars offer two mutually contradictory opinions on a legal problem or on the interpretation of a biblical verse, both opinions are considered to be "the words of the living God," since both are equally the result of a reverent search for an understanding of the Torah (Erub. 13b).

What was implicit in the rabbinic expansion of the concept of revelation must become an explicit principle in our day, when Jewish tradition faces the challenge of new ideas and of discoveries of major proportions. As a viable religion, Judaism must continue to be a vehicle of God's continuous Revelation to His people, for the voice that Israel heard at Sinai "did not cease" (Onkelos on Deut. 5:19).

—*Max Arzt*

THE SHOFAR: SALUTE TO THE SOVEREIGN

In the act of martyrdom, the power and grandeur of religion are brought to a focus. By dying for an ideal, the martyr makes death itself affirm the value of life and its power to cast off the evils that make life in the present intolerable under the yoke of oppression and persecution. By defying death, the martyr deprives evil of its deadliest weapon, the power of intimidation. Let none compare the suicide with the martyr. (Cf. Gen. R. LXXII, 8; Aboda Zarah 18a, the answer of R. Hanina b. Teradion to his disciples; Baba Kama 61a, the comment on II Sam. 23:16.) The suicide welcomes death because he hates the world and cannot find God in it; the martyr because he loves the world and finds complete self-fulfillment in carrying out the will of God, though it involves his own destruction as an individual. To the suicide, death means a bankrupt's exemption from the discharge of life's responsibilities when these appear overwhelming; but to the martyr, death is a payment in full with all the resources that he commands.

The role of the martyr in history is significant from yet another angle. Not only does it represent the sanctification of life in defiance of death, but it also points to the assertion of individual faith against social pressure. The martyr comes into conflict with the collective will of his contemporary society as expressed in its authoritative institutions because he views those institutions as *memshelet zadon*, as the dominion of arbitrary power which must vanish like smoke before the advent of the Kingdom of God. As a devotee of those ideals which he feels *should* be authoritative, he is a subject of that Kingdom. The etymology of the term "martyr" is significant. It is derived from a Greek word meaning "witness." The martyr is one who feels that his whole life must bear testimony to the supreme value of his ideal and that,

175

if he surrendered his principles under pressure, his conduct would be a *hillul hashem,* a profanation of the name of God and a betrayal of His Kingdom. The Jew's crowning distinction is to be a witness to God. "Ye are My witnesses, saith the Lord, and I am God." "If you act as My witnesses, I am God," says the Midrash, "but if you do not act as My witnesses, I am not, so to speak, God."

The sounding of the *Shofar*, the most ancient rite in the observance of Rosh ha-Shanah, has been interpreted as a summons to the soul to present itself before the judgment seat of God. It has also been construed as the *teruat melek*, the salute to the Sovereign, with all its implications of fealty and allegiance. It has functioned, and should still function, in the life of the Jewish people as an invitation to the individual Jew to renew his oath of unqualified allegiance and loyalty to those ideals, the realization of which would convert human society into a Kingdom of God.

—Mordecai M. Kaplan

Throughout Jewish history, the peal of the Shofar has testified to the Jewish will to survive in the face of every attempt at suppression. Even when forbidden to sound the Shofar, Jews always found a way. The Mishnah speaks of cases where it was necessary literally to take the Shofar underground: "If the Shofar was blown in a cistern or in a cellar or into a large jar. . . " The authorities were forced to postpone the Shofar ritual of the Shaḥarit service until Musaf during the Roman persecutions (as we have seen in our discussion of "Rules for the Shofar and the Tekiot"). In the Middle Ages, whenever Jews were forbidden to blow the Shofar—as in Spain, Arabia and elsewhere—the *Ba'al Tokay'a* would often conceal himself in a pit or in a barrel or walk off into the fields so that the sound might be lost among the hills and valleys. In Yemen, Jews were for centuries forbidden to blow Shofar.

In Palestine itself, as late as 1946, Jews were still being arrested by British police for blowing the Shofar at the Wailing Wall in Jerusalem despite strict prohibition of public religious ceremonies at this site of Arab-Jewish friction. As a matter of fact, it was forbidden even to bring a religious object into the area under pain of heavy jail sentence. Yet each summer determined Jewish youths drew lots for the privilege of trying to outwit the police and smuggle the forbidden Shofar into the congested area at the end of Yom Kippur. Not a year went by without a successful attempt to sound the Shofar at Israel's holiest shrine on the most solemn of days.

During the War of Liberation in 1948 the Wailing Wall, like the rest of the Old City of Jerusalem, fell into the hands of Arab Jordan. Nevertheless Jews continue each Yom Kippur to ascend nearby Mt.

Zion, face the Western Wall and sound the Shofar. Indeed, on Rosh Hashanah of 1958 (5719), Israelis reported having heard the sounds of a Shofar coming from the Old City; it is presumed that this Shofar was sounded by British soldiers of the Jewish faith among the troops who had been rushed into Jordan during the preceding summer to bolster the regime of King Hussein.

When the state of Israel was officially proclaimed on May 14, 1948, unprecedented celebrations were touched off all over the Jewish world and the Shofar played its part in some of these observances. When the Knesset held its inaugural session, the arrival of President Chaim Weizmann to take the oath of office was heralded by the sounding of the Shofar; a similar rite marked the dedication of the new religious headquarters, *Hayḥal Shelomo*, in 1958. Thus the ancient ram's horn has helped to mark a new epoch in the age-old struggle for the restoration of Israel and Torah to the ancestral homeland. No more appropriate symbol could have been found to give voice to the Jewish will to live as a free nation and to shape its own destinies as the "People of the Covenant."

—Herman Kieval

Some time ago, a sheep-herder in the hills of Idaho sent a letter to one of the national radio programs in which he made a strange request. He explained that he listened to the program every week and that the radio was his sole companion in his lonely occupation. His old violin which he used to play was now so badly out of tune as to be worthless. "I wonder if you would be kind enough" he went on "to pause on your 10 o'clock program on Tuesday morning to strike an "A" so that I might tune my violin and enjoy its music again."

The shepherd's request was honored. On the 10 o'clock program the following Tuesday, the announcer read his unusual request to his nationwide audience and then an "A" was sounded so that the shepherd might tune his violin and play it again.

On Rosh Hashanah God bids us to sound an "A" on the Shofar so that each of us might tune up the instruments of our lives and proceed to play beautiful music.

—*Sidney Greenberg*

COMPOSING PRAYERS

Levi Isaac stood by the reader's table prepared to sound the *shofar*. The congregation waited patiently for him to commence. After a long interval, the sexton hesitatingly approached Levi Isaac and asked the cause for the delay.

The rabbi whispered to the sexton:

"A stranger is seated near the door of the synagogue. Reared among non-Jews, he never learned to pray. However, he has just said to God:

" 'Lord of the universe, You understand the true meaning of prayers and You know those that are most acceptable. Since I know only the letters of the alphabet, I shall repeat them and You can compose from them the prayers I should recite on this sacred day.'

"The Almighty is now preoccupied with composing prayers from the letters. Therefore, we must wait."

—The Rosh Hashanah Anthology

Rabbi David of Lelov was the regular *shofar*-blower at the synagogue of Rabbi Jacob Isaac, the Seer of Lublin. One Rosh Hashanah when the time arrived for the blowing of the *shofar* Rabbi David was not in the synagogue. The Seer of Lublin, who thought Rabbi David must be concentrating on solemn meditations for the *tekiot*, sent a disciple to look for him. After a wide search he found Rabbi David in the marketplace feeding horses. The disciple angrily said, "What's wrong with you? The Rabbi is waiting for you a long time and here you are feeding the horses!"

Rabbi David retorted, "I know that the Jewish wagon drivers are in the synagogue and they have undoubtedly forgotten to give fodder to their horses. So I went to feed them. After all, it is a duty to prevent cruelty to animals."

He then returned to the synagogue and blew the *shofar*. After he had finished the Seer of Lublin remarked, "Today Rabbi David entertained lofty sentiments before sounding the *shofar*."

CHOOSING A SHOFAR-BLOWER

Rabbi Levi Isaac was interrogating a number of candidates for the blowing of the *shofar* on Rosh Hashanah. He asked each one:

"What will be your thoughts while you blow the *shofar*?"

The Berditchever rabbi was dissatisfied with the variety of pious sentiments voiced by the candidates until one of them said:

"Rabbi, I'm a simple, poor Jew. I have four daughters who have long ago reached the marriage age but I am unable to provide dowries for them. When I will blow the *shofar*, I will bear my daughters in mind. I will think: 'Merciful One! I am fulfilling the commandments You have ordained. Give ear to the *shofar* sound beseeching You to fulfill your obligation of providing dowries for my daughters.'"

The straightforward, sincere honesty of this Jew appealed to Levi Isaac and he engaged him to sound the *shofar*.

The saintly Abraham Isaac Kook, late chief rabbi of
Israel, lay critically ill in the hospital. When the
month of Elul began, he asked that the *shofar* be
sounded each morning so that he might fulfill the
commandment of hearing the trumpet sounds during
this month preceding Rosh Hashanah. The doctor,
reluctant to comply with this request lest the blasts
have an adverse effect on the rabbi, vainly tried to
dissuade his patient. The rabbi insisted that the *shofar*
be blown.

Finally one of Rabbi Kook's pupils discreetly
suggested:

"If the *shofar* is sounded in the hospital, wouldn't
the other patients be disturbed?"

The pious sage immediately said:

"Maybe you are right. If that be so, do not blow
the *shofar*."

THE SHOFAR AT THE WESTERN WALL

The Western Wall of the Temple in Jerusalem was the object of friction between Arabs and Jews for many years. In 1929, as a gesture of appeasement to the Arabs, the British Mandatory government forbade the sounding of the *shofar* at the Western Wall at the conclusion of Yom Kippur, but the Jewish underground decided to ignore this prohibition.

As the *Neilah* service was being concluded with the cantor chanting the *Avinu Malkenu*, he interpolated the Hebrew verse, "Our Father, our King, we have the *shofar*; draw a circle around us." There was a momentary deep hush when suddenly, from one end of the wall, a tremulous but clear *shofar* sound clarioned from a child's voice. As the British police converged upon the child, a *tekiah gedolah* reverberated from the other end of the wall. Whereupon the assembled worshippers united in a spontaneous cry "Next year in Jerusalem rebuilt," and then burst out in singing *Hatikvah*."

The following year Moshe Segal, a watchman in the Galil, came to spend Yom Kippur in Jerusalem and to pray at the Western Wall. When the fast day ended he blew a *shofar* and was immediately arrested by the British. They held him at the police station without food until midnight, when he was released. Only then did he learn how his release was effected. The late chief rabbi of Palestine, Abraham Isaac Kook, when informed that Segal was arrested, phoned the secretary of the British administration and told him, "I have fasted all day but I will not eat until you will free the man who blew the *shofar*." "But the man violated a government order," the secretary replied. To which Rabbi Kook retorted, "He fulfilled a religious commandment." The rabbi's moral suasion prevailed, and the secretary promised to release Segal.

Year after year, despite the arrest of Jews, many of whom were disciples of Segal, ways were devised to outwit the British police and to conclude Yom Kippur according to tradition. When the Old City of Jerusalem became part of Jordan in 1948, Jews ascended Mount Zion adjacent to the Old City, and facing the Western Wall, they sounded the *shofar* to conclude the ritual of the holiest day of the year.

On June 7, 1967, when the Israel Defense Forces recaptured the Old City of Jerusalem and assembled at the Western Wall, the *shofar* was again sounded to proclaim the victory and to reassert the right of the Jews to worship in freedom at their most sacred site. At the end of Yom Kippur that year Moshe Segal, at the request of Minister Menahem Beigin, was given the distinction of being the first to sound the *shofar*.

—Tuviah Preshel

Rabbi Shlomoh Goren, chief of chaplains of the Israel Defense Forces, advised soldiers near enemy bases that they were exempt from listening to the sounds of the *shofar*, so that their locations might not be betrayed.